Aligning with

HEAVEN

A PRACTICAL GUIDE TO SPIRITUAL WARFARE

Removing obstacles in your life
so you can become
the Bride of Christ

WRITTEN BY: KELLY CRUMPLEY
EDITED BY: CRESTA OGLE

Acknowledgements

First, I'd like to thank my ABBA Father in Heaven who gave me this project and equipped me to complete it. Without Your personal teaching, revelation, encouragement, and giving of spiritual gifts, I would be teaching from a theological standpoint and not by personal experience. I would have never thought someone like me could be following Jesus and be sharing the good news of the Gospel; what an AWESOME God you are!

I'd like to thank my husband David for being such a support and encouragement to me. Thank you for buying me so many Bible Study books (and finally a Kindle when our bookshelf ran out of space), for letting me devote my life to my ABBA Father, for asking hard questions and challenging me, and for always holding me accountable to seek God's approval on everything I do – even if you think it sounds crazy. How blessed I am to be your wife.

I want to say "Thank you!" to Cresta Ogle for editing my writings. You are amazing and have been a huge encouragement to me in more ways than you'll ever know. I also want to thank my daughters, Paige and Taylor, and my son, Parker, who is an amazing little prayer warrior! I am grateful for all of you who have prayed over this project: Jessica Goldsmith, Beth Tigert, Amanda Pearson, and many others. I am also forever thankful for all the people listed in the back of this book who have inspired me with your passion for the Word.

TABLE OF CONTENTS

INTRODUCTION

The Bride of Christ

The Bride of Christ is a Christian who walks intimately with God. She probably once was broken in so many pieces that she thought life was an endless, painful, hopeless struggle. She strived to measure-up but never quite made it. She knew there was more to herself than what she expressed. Then she made her heart right with God, repented of her sin, and came under His authority. God forgave all her sins and took away her guilt and shame. She is now clothed in white which represents the righteousness of Christ. She is dead to her old way of life and to the world, but alive by the Spirit of God. She experiences the supernatural love, fellowship, and abundant life that God offers. She puts nothing above her relationship with God. Because God is number one, He blesses her in every area of her life. No blessing is more valuable to her than the relationship between herself and her Husband, Jesus Christ. She has every spiritual gift and sees healing miracles and people being freed from demonic attachments every day. She seeks to please her Husband and no other. Because she wants to please God, she reaches out and touches the broken-hearted, the poor, and the crippled. She heals them all and brings them into the Kingdom. She overflows with the joy of the Lord and spreads His goodness wherever she goes. She speaks on His behalf and brings peace to the people of the world.

If I had to describe the topic of this book in two words it would be: faith and authority. These are two areas where God is moving powerfully within the Body of Christ. I believe that it is God's purpose for this book to specifically address these two areas. As God was preparing me to pen the pages of this book, I was personally challenged greatly in these two areas. Do I *really* have faith in God? Am I *really* walking like Jesus? Do I truly believe what the Bible says about my life? What I realized was that, no, I didn't really trust Him like I should. I needed to get past my unbelief and live by faith. So I wondered, "Since I don't have faith, how do I get it?" Then I had a revelation that changed everything for me!

Consequently, faith comes from hearing the message, and the message is heard through the word about Christ. Romans 10:17

So if faith comes by hearing the message about Christ, then I needed to hear more of God's Word. To me, that meant immersing myself in hearing the Word of God (by reading and listening to faith-filled sermons), and also hearing from God directly. Your life will be transformed if you do these two things, just as mine was, and just like millions of others have been. No one can convince you to have faith. You have to find it on your own. It is a gift from God. You've got to learn how to receive the gift, and the first step is believing that God wants you to have it. Once you get just a little bit of faith, even as small as a mustard seed, everything changes!

When we have faith, we can do anything. We can have salvation, we can live in victory, we can experience healing, and we can walk on water. *Without* faith, we may have a theoretical idea of the theology of God, but not an intimate experience with Him. We need to have faith that God will do what He has promised, whether it makes sense to us or not. Faith is the vehicle God uses to demonstrate His love for us! We need not merely hope, but have perfect faith. Hope means we accept that it might not happen. We just *hope* it will happen. Faith means we *know* for sure that it is God's will for us. In order to know that, we need to hear His word which is filled with the answers we are seeking.

> *Jesus looked at them and said, "With man this is impossible, but not with God; all things are possible with God." Mark 10:27*

When we have perfect faith, we break down the barriers between us and God's will for us. We can then experience God's amazing, supernatural love for us and the goodness and joy that can come through only Him!

> *He replied, "Because you have so little faith. Truly I tell you, if you have faith as small as a mustard seed, you can say to this mountain, 'Move from here to there,' and it will move. Nothing will be impossible for you." Matthew 17:20*

These are amazing words that Jesus spoke! We all have mountains in our lives. These mountains are things that we let overwhelm us, distract us, and zap our energy. These are the things that have control over our time that we wish didn't. These are things that we battle and ask God to take away, but we feel like He isn't answering our prayers. These *things* are obstacles to us living in

God's perfect will, and obstacles that God gave us authority to eliminate from our lives! We need to take a little responsibility and walk with the authority that God gave us. We are allowing these mountains to control us so much that we are living in fear. God doesn't want us to live in fear, but to live in victory! We are supposed to be so heavenly-minded that we laugh in the face of our enemy. We are chosen, called out, and anointed by God to proclaim the Good News!

Now this I know: The Lord gives victory to his anointed. He answers him from his heavenly sanctuary with the victorious power of his right hand. Psalm 20:6

Being anointed refers to the practice of putting oil upon one's head and being consecrated, blessed, ordained, and made holy. Oil represents the Holy Spirit of God. Holy means *dedicated* to God. When you enter into the Kingdom of God you are anointed and receive the Holy Spirit as proof of your sonship. You have been *called out* of the world and called to *enter into* the Body of Christ. If you aren't feeling that you're anointed, get some oil and anoint yourself! Apply some oil to your forehead, and pray Ephesians 6:3-12:

Praise be to the God and Father of our Lord Jesus Christ, who has blessed us in the heavenly realms with every spiritual blessing in Christ. For he chose us in him before the creation of the world to be holy and blameless in his sight. In love he predestined us for adoption to sonship through Jesus Christ, in accordance with his pleasure and will— to the praise of his glorious grace, which he has freely given us in the One he loves. In him we have redemption through his blood, the forgiveness of sins, in accordance with the riches of God's grace that he lavished on us. With all wisdom and understanding, he made known to us the mystery of his will according to his good pleasure, which he purposed in Christ, to be put into effect when the times reach their fulfillment—to bring unity to all things in heaven and on earth under Christ. In him we were also chosen, having been predestined according to the plan of him who works out everything in conformity with the purpose of his will, in order that we, who were the first to put our hope in Christ, might be for the praise of his glory. Amen!

I started wondering about the anointing and about being the Bride of Christ after I was saved and began reading the Bible. A part of me thought that I wasn't worthy of such a blessing, but the invitation was still beckoning me whenever I read God's Word. I had the feeling that God was really hoping I would accept His marriage proposal! Once I got past my shortcomings and realized that God truly desired an intimate, deeper, all-consuming relationship with me, I was so delighted to accept!

As a young man marries a young woman, so will your Builder marry you; as a bridegroom rejoices over his bride, so will your God rejoice over you.
Isaiah 62:5

Once I accepted, it was like any other love story, and all I wanted to do was spend time with God. I fell in love with Jesus! I'm so crazy about Him that I've changed my whole life to please Him. He is so worthy of praise and admiration. How He loves us so! My favorite things to do all include Him. How could anything possibly compare? But then I started noticing that many believers did not have this kind of relationship with Him, and I wondered, "How can such an awesome God not be your number-one squeeze?"

Knowing that I am loved and admired by God is the foundation of my faith – the proof of that love is Jesus. I know God loves me because He sent His Son to die for me. How much more can you show your love for someone? What passion He has for us! I am filled with God's love and it overflows to others. I can't help it; if I don't share God's love I feel like I might explode! God works His love through me often with supernatural miracles that dramatically change people's lives. People call me weird, and that's really okay with me. People misunderstand my motives because they've never allowed themselves to experience God's love before. His love is so perfect that I can even be nice to people who are mean to me and still feel good.

There are about a million reasons that we can find to be offended by people's behavior; but love says, "No, you don't!". How can we be offended by people who don't know any better because they don't know the love of God? If they knew how much God loved them, they wouldn't do or say any of those things. The Holy Spirit makes it possible to love without measure. I want you to be filled with this overflowing measure of love. It is so life-changing to feel really loved by God. It's not a narcissistic love of self, but rather, a humbling love through which you see yourself and others as God sees us. He views us with compassion and grace.

God offers the oil of anointing as a gift to those who repent and turn to Him. The people that use the oil and live by the Spirit and Truth are who will be invited into the wedding chamber. These people know their King and know the blessings and authority that has been given to them. They are used by God in miraculous ways to bring light into the darkness. Some people are simply consecrated and set aside, never knowing their King intimately. But some stay awake, alert, focused on their God, and God rewards them with His intimate Presence and all of the heavenly blessings in Christ!

"At that time the kingdom of heaven will be like ten virgins who took their lamps and went out to meet the bridegroom. Five of them were foolish and five were wise. The foolish ones took their lamps but did not take any oil with them. The wise ones, however, took oil in jars along with their lamps. The bridegroom was a long time in coming, and they all became drowsy and fell asleep. "At midnight the cry rang out: 'Here's the bridegroom! Come out to meet him!' "Then all the virgins woke up and trimmed their lamps. The foolish ones said to the wise, 'Give us some of your oil; our lamps are going out.' "'No,'

they replied, 'there may not be enough for both us and you. Instead, go to those who sell oil and buy some for yourselves.' "But while they were on their way to buy the oil, the bridegroom arrived. The virgins who were ready went in with him to the wedding banquet. And the door was shut. "Later the others also came. 'Lord, Lord,' they said, 'open the door for us!' "But he replied, 'Truly I tell you, I don't know you.' "Therefore keep watch, because you do not know the day or the hour."
Matthew 25:1-13

The virgins represent Christians. We see in this parable that only half of them went into the wedding banquet. The ones that kept watch and had their oil (remember this represents the Holy Spirit) were allowed to enter. The door was closed to those that didn't have the oil. We need to live by the leading of the Holy Spirit so we can enter into God's presence and experience the abundant life in the Promised Land that is His perfect will for us. Living in God's Presence is a place that we choose to live, spiritually, and from that place, we become a fountain of living water through which God shows His love to the world.

Perfect Will vs. Permissive Will

Our ABBA Father desires that we align ourselves with the Kingdom of Heaven and live in His *perfect will*. Many of us are simply walking in God's *permissive will*, not reaching our full potential by walking in God's *perfect will*. God's *perfect will* is the narrow path where you walk and live perfectly united with the will of God. Yeshua

viii

(Jesus's original Hebrew name) is the only person who has ever done it. But, nevertheless, it is the goal to which we aspire as children of God.

Do not conform to the pattern of this world, but be transformed by the renewing of your mind. Then you will be able to test and approve what God's will is—his good, pleasing and perfect will. Romans 12:2

God's *permissive will* is where we believe *in God* but we don't *believe God.* Our thinking doubts God on so many levels that it's an embarrassment to our King! Even the devil believes in God. The devil knows God is real and that He has triumphed over him. When Yeshua (Jesus) was resurrected, all the power the enemy had on this earth was removed. Yeshua (Jesus) took the keys of power from the devil and gave it to the "church," the "called out ones," the "anointed ones." Jesus gave the authority over the enemy to us! When we are not recognizing the enemy and standing firm on the word of God, things will happen to us which God allows, but it is not His *perfect will* for us.

This is where spiritual warfare comes in. The only power the enemy has against us is the power we give him. He attacks us because we doubt God and decide to believe the devil's lies instead of God's Truth. We "invite" the enemy into our lives because we agree that what he tells us is real, instead of believing God. We know that Yeshua (Jesus) died for us, but we forget that He rose again and gave us life! He gave us the keys to the Kingdom of God!

The storehouses of heaven are waiting for us to realize who we are so we can be God's hands and feet to take back this world from a defeated enemy. The war is won but there is ground that must be re-claimed. At one point or another, every Christian needs to know how to recognize when it is the enemy leading and when it is God leading. In the next few chapters, we are going to see how our behaviors line up. Do they mimic the personality of Hassatan (Satan's original Hebrew name), or do they mimic the personality of Yeshua (Jesus)? By the way, you'll also be learning a bit of Hebrew as an added bonus (no extra charge!).

ABBA wants us to live in the Spirit and not by the flesh. God wants us to realize our inheritance and walk with His authority. Just doing Christian things by the work of the flesh doesn't make you a Christian. Reciting a prayer once doesn't make you a Christian. Our salvation is not as easy as we have been taught to believe. Our salvation was so difficult to achieve that God Himself had to do it! We should be very careful to humble ourselves before our God and know that He loves us so much, that He sent Yeshua (Jesus) to die in our place. Once we were slaves to sin, but what are we now?

You have been set free from sin and have become slaves to righteousness. Romans 6:18

This means that if we are Christians, we ought to have a life change that makes us yearn for righteousness. We need to be "born again." We should have a life that reflects a movement towards holiness, in addition to the supernatural workings of the Holy Spirit. The Holy Spirit that resides within us will work to refine our character, and will confirm God to others by His supernatural outpouring of love.

Then the disciples went out and preached everywhere, and the Lord worked with them and confirmed his word by the signs that accompanied it.
Mark 16:20

If we are Christians, we seek to be continually filled with the Holy Spirit and depend on it. We need to become aware of our sinful selves so that we are humble to God and compassionate towards others who are also made in His image. When we are filled with God's love and acceptance, that love will overflow into all our relationships. Fear, unbelief and insecurity have no place in us because *in Christ* we are *in* His perfect love.

There is no fear in love. But perfect love drives out fear, because fear has to do with punishment. The one who fears is not made perfect in love.
1 John 4:18

Our lives are not the same when we are continually seeking guidance by the Holy Spirit and studying His Word so that we may test and approve God's *perfect will*. When we walk in the Spirit, God works through us using the spiritual gifts, giving us power and spiritual authority over the enemy so that we may bring glory to God and usher others into the Kingdom.

It is not our power that is at work, but God's power through the Holy Spirit. I will warn you, though, there are many who profess to be Christians that do not live by the leading of the Holy Spirit. These are people who love God and volunteer their time, but may have never been filled with the Holy Spirit. These people are walking on the bridge of salvation, but never enter into the Promised Land. The road that leads to the Promised Land is only found by the leading of the Holy Spirit.

Enter through the narrow gate. For wide is the gate and broad is the road that leads to destruction, and many enter through it. But small is the gate and narrow the road that leads to life, and only a few find it. Matthew 7:13-14

Many Christians know little of the Holy Spirit and have never been baptized in water or by the Spirit. Leading polls say that 59% of professing Christians don't agree that Satan or the Holy Spirit are living beings[1]. God is a supernatural being. His supernatural workings are through the Holy Spirit. God always used supernatural workings to confirm Himself in the Old Testament, and He did this also to confirm Yeshua's (Jesus's) ministry in the New Testament. But that doesn't mean that every supernatural working is from God. We are warned that in latter times the enemy will also have supernatural workings and that many will be deceived. The Bible tells us exactly how to spot the deception; these people will have the workings of supernatural power, but they will not live by God's law. They will lead people to worship them instead of pointing them to the Lord Jesus Christ.

Don't let anyone deceive you in any way, for that day will not come until the rebellion occurs and the

---

[1] Barna Group. "Most American Christians Do Not Believe That Satan or the Holy Spirit Exist." *Barna.org*. Barna Group, 13th Apr. 2009. Web. 15th Apr. 2016.

man of lawlessness is revealed, the man doomed to destruction. 2 Thessalonians 2:3

Yeshua (Jesus) came to give us salvation so we can enter into the Kingdom of God and walk obediently by the Spirit of God. Following God's law and the Ten Commandments won't earn us salvation, but is a byproduct of obedience from living by the Spirit. We should be sensitive to the leading of the Holy Spirit, and cringe when we step out of alignment with God's laws and perfect will for us. Jesus tells us that if we love God first and love our neighbor as ourselves we will fulfill the law. In order to truly love God first, we need to make Him first in our lives. In order to love our neighbor as ourselves, we need God's supernatural love to do it. Living morally is not enough. It is by fear and trembling that we work out our salvation and obedience to God, and a daily battle to align ourselves with God's perfect will. This road is narrow because we need to fear God more than we fear the judgments of man. There are so many people that are truly seeking love and are looking in all the wrong places. We need to show them God's amazing love by seeking out a deeper relationship with Him ourselves so that we can, in turn, pour out His love for them.

Examine Yourself

Do you know for sure where you are going when your life ends on this earth? Do you know *for sure* that you are "saved"? How do you know? Because you believe? How do you know you believe? Is there fruit in your life? Is God number one in your life? Does your life show it, or is it merely a verbal statement of faith? Are you being refined into the image of Yeshua (Jesus)? Is there any proof of that? Have you become so aware of your sinfulness that you can do nothing but ask the Holy Spirit for words to speak and for how to treat others? Do you think of others as higher than yourself and treat others lovingly, no matter what? Do you live free from guilt, fear, and shame? Do you experience God's presence on a regular basis? The love for God in a believer's life will show in the way they live; they will have an attitude of thankfulness.

Three Obstacles to Your Relationship to God

There are three main obstacles that stand between you and intimate fellowship with God: *the world,* which wages war against us (our ungodly culture); our own *sinful nature* (flesh); and our *adversary,* Hassatan (Satan) and his demons. This book is designed to help you analyze your life and bring it into alignment with God's perfect will so you can experience victory over all three areas. We can be more than conquerors when we are *in Christ.* We are seated with Christ in heavenly places and are called to live a life worthy of that calling. We do not want to be ignorant of the things that are working against us, but rather, we need to focus on the one who overcame, Yeshua (Jesus). God wants us to constantly be growing and maturing in our faith, growing in love and helping to cultivate a life of faith in others. You do not need to have white hair to be a mature Christian, but you should know the basic principals of the Gospel and be eagerly searching for more solid food.

But solid food is for the mature, who by constant use have trained themselves to distinguish good from evil. Hebrews 5:14

Knowing good and evil isn't something that comes naturally. It takes time and training to successfully distinguish between the two. This level of understanding isn't just for people who are "super-spiritual." It's for those that hunger and thirst for more of God. There are only four things you really need to have in order to be successful in spiritual warfare:

1. Willingness to Listen to and Obey God
2. Knowing Your Identity in Christ
3. Dependence on God
4. Courage to Make Change

Willingness to Listen to and Obey God

God wants us to spend ample time with Him, listening to Him, reading His word, praying, worshipping, earnestly seeking the spiritual gifts (1 Corinthians 12), and desiring to receive personal revelations from Him (Revelation is where God *reveals* information to you.). He also wants us to follow through and obey what He tells us, not just listen to what He says and then let it go in one ear and out the other. He confirms His word to us by two or three witnesses, so we must develop hearing ears that understand God's perfect will.

Whoever has ears, let them hear what the Spirit says to the churches. To the one who is victorious, I will

give the right to eat from the tree of life, which is in
the paradise of God. Revelation 2:7

Knowing Your Identity in Christ

Our ABBA Father wants us to *desire* to be conformed into the image of Yeshua Hamashiach (Jesus Christ). To be victorious over the enemies you face, you need to know your true identity as a member of the Kingdom of God. You are "born again" by the incorruptible seed of God, are from heaven and are heavenly bound, and are living temporarily on this fallen earth working towards a life that imitates Yeshua (Jesus).

Therefore, if anyone is in Christ, the new creation
has come: The old has gone, the new is here!
2 Corinthians 5:17

God wants you to truly see yourself as a new creation; you've got to let the past be the past and walk forward with child-like faith in God and His word. The enemy will first try to get you to doubt God and then yourself. This is what Hassatan (Satan) did to Adam and Eve thousands of years ago, and the tactic still works today. If you are born again, you are clean and washed and reign with Christ in heavenly places. All authority over your spiritual foes is given to you as your inheritance. You lack no good thing when your purpose and mind are set on the things of God.

Dependence on God

Dependence on God is being at the point where you realize you don't have it all figured out, and that
xvi

God does. In particular, it's being at that point where you can praise Him even when times are tough, and that you can also separate yourself from the world and devote yourself to God when things are going well.

Our whole lives should be built on the leading of Yeshua (Jesus), and not just from what we learn from other people. Everything that goes into our mind needs to be sifted through the mind of Christ. There is so much deception in the world, even in Christianity, that we are being called as the Body of Christ to restore the truth of God's Word and follow Him wholeheartedly.

See to it that no one takes you captive through hollow and deceptive philosophy, which depends on human tradition and the elemental spiritual forces of this world rather than on Christ. Colossians 2:8

It probably means for many people that you get off Facebook and get your face in the Book (The Bible)! When we depend on God for comfort, counsel, direction, and insight, we can be sure that what we receive from Him is beneficial. People are just not capable of giving us the kind of support we need to fulfill God's purpose for our lives. We are invited to put our trust and faith in God in all areas of our life.

Courage to Make Change

The last main component you'll need is courage. It takes courage to face your own fears and break down the walls that have kept you from succeeding. We need to be humble before God and boldly go where He leads us. We can't be worried about what people will think about us. There are so many suffering people in the world and your light is meant to shine into the darkness! Not everyone needs to agree with you, but as long as you are acting in love and being led by Yeshua (Jesus), you will have the armies of heaven behind you. You will be persecuted not because they reject you, but because they reject the One who sent you. Sometimes the truth hurts, and you need to know how to speak the truth in love. When you stand boldly for something, there will be people who have differing opinions, and that is okay. People will often misunderstand your motives and think that your good works are for self-promotion. Some people have doubts and fears and just aren't there yet, but you can still love them.

It took personal experience for me to believe in the supernatural workings of God. Many don't believe God still heals people, but I know for sure that He does because I've seen healing miracles. There are many who don't believe in demons or evil spirits, but I know for sure that they exist because I've seen people delivered from them. There are also people who don't believe that Yeshua (Jesus) is the Son of God and that He still lives today, but I know for sure because I've seen Him and know Him personally!

Be strong and courageous. Do not be afraid or terrified because of them, for the Lord your God goes with you; he will never leave you nor forsake you.
Deuteronomy 31:6

There are a lot of people who are still blinded by the enemy and you can't let it negatively affect your faith in God. God doesn't want you to fear anything. God is with you always, and no weapon formed against you will prevail. Being courageous means picking yourself up when you fall and leaning on the power of God, spending time in His presence, receiving everything you need from Him. Yeshua (Jesus) is seated at the right hand of God, and we are seated with Him when we are *in Christ*.

Since, then, you have been raised with Christ, set your hearts on things above, where Christ is, seated at the right hand of God. Colossians 3:1

I encourage you to pray regularly as we go through this study for: a softened heart, ears that hear, eyes that see (spiritually), and for personal revelation. Without revelation through the Holy Spirit, the Bible is simply a theological book. There will be plenty of people at the wedding banquet, but only a few who enter the wedding chamber. There are only a few who live by the Spirit *and* in Truth. These are the believers who are close enough to Him to be called His Bride.

CHAPTER 1

Our Spiritual Foes

Our battles are not against flesh and blood (or persons with bodies), but in the invisible realm. We love all people because we are all created in the image of God. We battle simply against the spiritual beings that influence people to sometimes do terrible things. Our hope is that all people will be filled by the Holy Spirit and walk in the light of God's love.

For our struggle is not against flesh and blood, but against the rulers, against the authorities, against the powers of this dark world and against the spiritual forces of evil in the heavenly realms. Ephesians 6:12

The battle begins in the mind, just like it did from the very beginning when Satan caused Eve to doubt God. We need to know God and His Word, (the Bible), in order to successfully overcome the enemy. The devil is a liar, and his power was taken at the cross. The enemy only has power if we give it to him. We stand firmly on the Word of God, and each of us needs to learn it for ourselves. We have all the tools we need to study the Bible. We can easily cross reference Scripture, read commentaries, compare hundreds of translations, participate in free online Bible Courses, watch sermons on YouTube, quickly look up dictionary words, attend conferences, and more.

With the printing press and the internet, an entire generation has been blessed to be able to not just *read* the Bible, but to really research it. I have to admit this has become my #1 passion over the past several years. What has been revealed to me by God and confirmed by Scripture is that we are in a spiritual battle that has been going on for thousands of years. We are a part of something much larger than ourselves. A personal relationship with God combined with the study of Scripture has allowed me to become familiar with the "voice" of God. It has become easier with experience to recognize when God is giving me direction and when the enemy is trying to imitate God and push me off-track.

> *A personal relationship with God combined with the study of Scripture has allowed me to become familiar with the "voice" of God.*

Shortly after I was "born again", I experienced several spiritual attacks by the enemy. He tried to rip my family apart and make me believe that God didn't care about me. I was totally desperate, and that was when I decided to really make Jesus Lord and King of my life. I said, "God, I give you all the broken pieces of my life. It's all I have to give. I've screwed everything up. I'm waiting for you to tell me what to do next. I know there has to be more. Whatever you want for me is what I want. I don't have any expectations; put me where you need me." Three days passed and I was miserable, alone and without direction.

I waited desperately to hear from God. I picked up the Bible and started reading. I turned on Christian music and worshipped Him through my tears. On the third night, an angel of the Lord came to my room, and God gave me a vision and a prophecy! His presence filled the room, and I could see the outline of His shape, but He was translucent. I was able to talk to the angel without speaking; it was some kind of telepathic communication. The angel showed me what God was doing *through people* to overcome the evil in the world. He said there would be a changing tide in the media and that there would be surge of Bible-related movies, shows, and news stories. God showed me that I was going to be a part of it, and that I would write books for Him and be involved with the media. God wanted me to teach and preach the Gospel, and to specifically teach people about angels and spiritual warfare. I thought to myself, "I don't know anything! I'm just learning. What could I teach?" The angel seemed to sense my thoughts. Then the angel asked me if I wanted to accept God's plan. I still wondered how I would be able to accomplish any of the things in the vision, but I answered, "Yes, Father, I will do it, but you are going to have to help me!" It was the most incredible experience.

I started wondering what Bible College I would need to attend in order to be a Bible teacher, and as if He read my mind, He replied, "No college. I will teach you. I will validate you myself. You will be qualified because I said so!" What could be a higher honor than being ordained by God Himself to teach? You may not recognize me as a teacher based on the world's standards, but God does, so you should too. God showed me three Scriptures to encourage me on this anointing:

Don't let anyone look down on you because you are young, but set an example for the believers in speech, in conduct, in love, in faith and in purity. 1 Timothy 4:12

But you are a chosen people, a royal priesthood, a holy nation, God's special possession, that you may declare the praises of him who called you out of darkness into his wonderful light. 1 Peter 2:9

25

But God chose the foolish things of the world to shame the wise; God chose the weak things of the world to shame the strong. 1 Corinthians 1:27

I certainly felt like a "foolish thing" at the time this vision and prophecy was given to me. God wants to give spiritual gifts to all those that seek Him and ask, but it is Christ in us who will overcome the darkest spiritual forces. We need wisdom and discernment from God. The supernatural power and knowledge the Holy Spirit gives us is of immeasurable worth. We need to be continuously tapping into God with a hunger and thirst which are always growing.

Prayer for Wisdom and Knowledge

Father God, I ask that you would give me wisdom and knowledge and the spirit of revelation so that I may understand your Word. I ask to have eyes that see spiritually, ears that hear Your message, and a pure heart that accepts Your truth. Thank you, Jesus! Amen.

Part of the vision that God showed me also included a view of this generation and that people are starting to turn to God. Since that vision in 2011, things have definitely started to change. Even though the darkness seems to be getting darker, God's people are getting brighter, and even the media is having an explosion of Bible-related movies, documentaries, and other films. Historical groups are conducting massive world-wide archeological studies in attempts to verify the Bible with convincing results. Stories from the Old Testament which are considered by people today as "myths" are being re-evaluated as actual historical events. For example, the Battle of Jericho was excavated and the only standing wall was found in the exact spot described in the Bible as where Rahab lived, which was the only wall God permitted to let stand. There is also evidence that the city burned and that all the walls fell at the same time. Kind of interesting, don't you think?

It is important for you to grasp that there are awesome, supernatural things that God is doing in this generation. There are awesome miracles that Jesus performed in the New Testament which He wants us to do as well. I believe Jesus gave the blind their sight; I believe Jesus raised people from the dead; I believe He made the cripples walk; and I also believe that He delivered people and healed them. I know He still does these things because I have personally experienced His supernatural healing and power. I have accurately prophesied over people, and I have received information supernaturally about people that led to a growth of faith and in their physical healing. I also believe these words from Jesus apply to us today:

Very truly I tell you, whoever believes in me will do the works I have been doing, and they will do even greater things than these, because I am going to the Father.
John 14:12

Jesus says that we will do even greater things than He did! Isn't that wonderful? Whoever believes in Jesus will do even greater things. You can do greater things. In fact, I think something is stirring in you right now, deep within your belly telling you that this is meant for you. I think you want to do greater things, but you just don't know where to start. Well, for starters, you've got to make Jesus your High Priest and Teacher, and you need to receive the Holy Spirit. Everything you read must be verified with Scripture and/or with the Holy Spirit. Preferably both, but in some parts of this book I am giving you details based on experience and revelation, so you'll want to try and focus on the Scripture part and take my writings simply as a testimony to their truth.

Jesus said we are the salt of the earth, but too much salt is not good, so I've tried to make this a flavorful read without being so salty that you want to spit it out.

The things I'm teaching regarding God's Word are things that you'll have to verify through your own experience. You may or may not believe me, but I won't be offended at all if you check it out everything for yourself. In fact, I really *want* you to verify everything because I think it's better to get the message straight from God instead of hearing it through someone else. This book isn't the Bible, and I'm sure somewhere in here is something that is not quite explained the way God intended it to be. I am still human so a little grace is appreciated in advance. We are going to be talking about subjects that people don't generally like to talk about, so you might want to get comfortable talking to God about it since other people might get a little weird.

We are in a time when people don't want to really hear the truth about the spiritual realm and the "forces of evil". The enemy is having a great time messing with people, and they have no idea what is going on. Some call it trials, or claim that God is refining them, and many times this is absolutely true. God does discipline His children. But how do we know when it is God is disciplining us, or if there are demons tormenting us? God is sovereign, but He is not in control of everything. He's not in control of cancer killing people. He's not in control of people being abused and violated. He's not in control of what I decide to cook for dinner. In Genesis 1:28, Scripture says He created man to have dominion and rule over the earth.

God blessed them and said to them, "Be fruitful and increase in number; fill the earth and subdue it. Rule over the fish in

28

the sea and the birds in the sky and over every living creature that moves on the ground." Genesis 1:28

Satan took dominion from Adam and Eve in the Garden of Eden, but Jesus got our dominion back. This is why Jesus was able to cast out demons; they didn't have dominion any more. Through faith, we receive forgiveness of sins and are given the Holy Spirit, Christ in us. We have power over the enemy, and we need to know how to use it! If we think God is in control of every bad thing that happens to us, why would Christ need to come and deliver and heal people? How can we truly love God and believe He is good when there is so much suffering?

In our minds, we will always doubt God's goodness if we don't understand that we have an enemy who comes to steal, kill, and destroy. We need to know that God has promised us good things, and that He is a covenant God. He made a blood covenant through the blood of Jesus and God cannot lie or break His promises. It goes against the nature of God to break His promises. We need to study God's Word and know exactly what God promises us through the blood covenant of Jesus so we can stand against the enemy. The fact is, the enemy is already defeated, and we need to learn how to walk out our lives as faith-filled Christians and walk the way Jesus walked. God confirmed Jesus's ministry through signs and wonders, and He does the same for us. God is supernatural, and He wants us to experience His supernatural gifts and miracles every day!

We need to study God's Word and know exactly what God promises us through the blood covenant of Jesus so we can stand against the enemy.

God is preparing a people that are stronger than previous generations in regards to spiritual warfare. That means we need to align ourselves with God. You need to be "briefed" by God Himself and ask for revelation from Him directly about where we can serve. That doesn't mean going and asking your Pastor; it means sitting down and praying to God for personal revelation. Jesus died so that you can have direct access to the throne room. You can get your "orders" from God, exactly like I did! If you want to see things from God's perspective and be loyal to Him, He will give you a great reward. You must come to God with a pure heart and realize that the relationship with God is more important than any "stuff" God can give you.

The mystery of the Kingdom of God is so alluring. The more you know, the more you want to know. When you really touch God and hear Him and follow Him, seeing for yourself His perfection and trustworthiness and grasping just a glimpse of how great He is, your troubles in this world are hardly a bump in the road!

No matter where you are in the struggles of this life, having faith in God will help you through it and make you a spiritual warrior that accomplishes many great things. Jesus has overcome the world, and you can too. You just need to have faith in God! If you don't have faith, here's how you can get it:

Consequently, faith comes from hearing the message, and the message is heard through the word about Christ.
Romans 10:17

You need to hear from God and read His word. Then your faith will grow. Faith is the fuel that you'll need to accomplish all those "greater things". Have faith in GOD, not in people, not in stuff, and not in yourself. Christ in you is the hope of glory. Sometimes spiritual gifts aren't enough to overcome certain things – we need *Christ in us*!

Two Kingdoms

There are two spiritual kingdoms: God's Kingdom, and Satan's Kingdom- the Kingdom of Light (God's Kingdom), and the Kingdom of Darkness (Satan's Kingdom). There is truth, and there is deception. There is right, and there is wrong. We are given a choice, in the abundance of God's love toward us, to choose the Kingdom with which we associate. If you are on the fence, be careful, because it belongs to the devil. God is shaking the fence, and you need to choose one side or the other. Let me show you from Scripture the truth of the reality of the two kingdoms. Although spiritual beings are not always something we can see with our eyes, they are real and they are eternal.

"The Lord has established his throne in heaven, and his kingdom rules over all." Psalm 103:19

Satan doesn't really want you to know that God's Kingdom is more powerful than his, and he certainly doesn't want you to know how to use the power God has given you. When Jesus began his public ministry, He never sent anyone out preaching the Kingdom unless they had authority over evil spirits and the powers of darkness. ALL Jesus' followers had this authority. They had authority over EVERY sickness and disease, and over EVERY impure spirit. Their success was limited to their level of faith, which seemed to be lacking most of the time to the dismay of Jesus!

"Jesus went through all the towns and villages, teaching in their synagogues, proclaiming the good news of the kingdom and healing every disease and sickness."
Matthew 9:35

When Jesus began to exercise His God-given authority, people who did not believe said He was crazy. But to those who believed, they were healed and sought Jesus to help them. The religious leaders of His time accused Jesus of working under the power of the enemy. Jesus responded by asking why the enemy would work against himself. Jesus wasn't casting devils out of people and healing them by the power of the devil! That doesn't even make sense.

The Words of Jesus: *"If Satan is divided against himself, how can his kingdom stand? I say this because you claim that I drive out demons by Beelzebul." Luke 11:18*

We also note from this Scripture that Jesus points out how Satan has a kingdom. There are many kingdoms in the world, of course, especially throughout the historical times in which the Bible was written. Even today we have "kingdoms". Keep in mind, though, we are talking about spiritual kingdoms, and the Bible only specifies two spiritual kingdoms. Supernatural power is real, and comes from two sources: either God or Satan. If it doesn't come from God, it comes from the enemy. The story in Exodus where the magicians of pharaoh mimic a few of the first plagues show that evil can perform supernatural things too. This is also why God had to cause 10 plagues; God had to show mankind forever, that He is most powerful, and that God's supernatural power is stronger than any kind of magic or sorcery.

We need to understand that Satan has a primary objective: to be worshipped above God. Satan comes to steal, kill, and destroy the lives of God's children. We better know what it is we are facing. God has given us the tools, and Jesus gave us the authority over the power of the devil. It is not God's will that we should suffer. Of course, God can take every bad thing the devil does and use it for good, but it is never God's will that His children should struggle and despair. Those that are under Satan's dominion, however, are not under God's blessings or protection.

"In which you used to live when you followed the ways of this world and of the ruler of the kingdom of the air, the spirit who is now at work in those who are disobedient."
Ephesians 2:2

Ephesians talks about a "ruler of the kingdom of the air", who is at work in those who are disobedient to God. Paul is talking to believers about how they now live a new life, but reminds them Satan is still at work in those that have not repented and turned to God. Here again we see that Satan has a kingdom, and that it is "working" in those that are disobedient to God, believers and non-believers alike. As believers, we are expected to be obedient.

"Or do you not know that wrongdoers will not inherit the kingdom of God? Do not be deceived: Neither the sexually immoral nor idolaters nor adulterers nor men who have sex with men, nor thieves nor the greedy nor drunkards nor slanderers nor swindlers will inherit the kingdom of God."
1 Corinthians 6:9-10

The New Testament (2 Timothy 3:5) warns that in the latter times, there will be believers with a form of godliness, but they will deny the power of God. The "power" of God is the supernatural workings of the Holy Spirit which include healing miracles, prophecy, deliverance, and the spiritual gifts. This type of believer is just like the Pharisees of old who follow laws and rituals and love to be known and greeted by sinners, but their inward lives are lacking, and they are not living by faith and are not empowered by God. Jesus says that many will claim to know

Him, but in reality, they do not know Him. They believe in Him but are unwilling to submit to His authority and His leading in their lives. They may even go to church and be involved with missionary work, but they are not doing God's will.

Doing good deeds without God's leading isn't necessarily the will of God. For too long, Christians have longed to please God and have gone out and done good deeds in their communities, trying to act like Christians instead of seeking an intimate relationship. These are simply works of the flesh, and are not of the Spirit. These people never enter the Promised Land, but are stuck on the bridge of salvation- receiving forgiveness, but never being filled with the Holy Spirit and entering into His presence, and into the life the resurrection gave us.

God wants us to be obedient to Him. That is where we align ourselves with His will and experience heaven on earth. Obedience is a theme you will see repeated throughout this book. This is the key to building a strong relationship with God. Hearing from the Holy Spirit, the Spirit of Truth, will guide you to fulfill your true purpose in life.

But when He, the Spirit of Truth, comes, He will guide you into all the truth. He will not speak on his own; He will speak only what He hears (from the Father), and He will tell you what is yet to come. John 16:13

Our Heavenly Father wants to speak with us. He wants us to hear His voice and obey Him. When we realize what we have in Christ, we can transform the world. God works through us, the temples of His Spirit, to accomplish great things.

CHAPTER 2

Partnering with Heaven

A Discerning Heart

When God gives you a discerning heart, it is the greatest of all heavenly gifts. Without a discerning heart, we cannot understand anything that comes from the Spirit of God. It is the pre-requisite to all other spiritual gifts and blessings from God.

The person without the Spirit does not accept the things that come from the Spirit of God but considers them foolishness, and cannot understand them because they are discerned only through the Spirit. 1 Corinthians 2:14

To *discern* is to perceive or recognize something. It is the ability to distinguish between Godly things and everything else. Our ability to follow the Holy Spirit is based on our discernment of what God is telling us to do. When we have a discerning heart, we are able to hear in our hearts when God is speaking to us. We've got to cultivate this skill because our spiritual growth is dependent on us hearing from God. You can read a hundred books and go to a dozen revival seminars, but things still might not make sense unless you have a discerning heart! A discerning heart is like the eyes of our souls that see into the heavenly spiritual realm. With time, we can discern not only the Holy Spirit, but other spirits as well.

When you meet another Christian, you know right away because the Holy Spirit senses itself in the other person. You can sense that you are like-minded because you are both part of the Body of Christ. You feel an instant sense of brother-sisterhood! You can also sense where that person is in their walk with God, whether they are new Christians or mature in their faith. I can even sense when someone has fallen asleep or when they have fallen away, and God will give me the perfect words to bring them back to Him. It's not something you can explain or learn anywhere; it just takes practice. It's kind of like learning to ride a bike. You just have to do it. This heightened awareness isn't something you master overnight, either. It takes deliberate focus on your part. God is the Giver of the gift of a discerning heart, but you have to take the steps and cultivate it in your life. If you don't put it into practice, you won't know how to do it. Just as with a bicycle, someone can give you a really nice bike, but if you never get on it and start pedaling, what is the point?

God is the Giver of the gift of a discerning heart, but you have to take the steps and cultivate it in your life.

Having the ability to discern things is also going to allow you to grow in wisdom. Wisdom isn't helpful unless you can discern and understand how to apply it. Discernment is how Jesus was able to perfectly minister to so many people. He developed His hearing heart and could hear exactly what God wanted to say to that person, and Jesus knew exactly how to present the message. He could receive a word of knowledge about a person and know exactly what to share. It wasn't that He was psychic, as this is from the realm of darkness. But God is all-knowing, and God wanted to show Jesus certain things so that He could connect with His people. In the following Biblical account, we read about a time when God gave special wisdom so that Jesus could connect and glorify God.

Now Jesus learned that the Pharisees had heard that he was gaining and baptizing more disciples than John— although in fact it was not Jesus who baptized, but his disciples. So he left Judea and went back once more to Galilee. Now he had to go through Samaria. So he came to a town in Samaria called Sychar, near the plot of ground Jacob had given to his son Joseph. Jacob's well was there, and Jesus, tired as he was from the journey, sat down by the well. It was about noon. When a Samaritan woman came to draw water, Jesus said to her, "Will you give me a drink?" (His disciples had gone into the town to buy food.) The Samaritan woman said to him, "You are a Jew and I am a Samaritan woman. How can you ask me for a drink?" (For Jews do not associate with Samaritans. Jesus answered her, "If you knew the gift of God and who it is that asks you for a drink, you would have asked him and he would have given you living water." "Sir," the woman said, "you have nothing to draw with and the well is deep. Where can you get this living water? Are you greater than our father Jacob, who gave us the well and drank from it himself, as did also his sons and his livestock?" Jesus answered, "Everyone who drinks this water will be thirsty again, but whoever drinks the water I give them will never thirst. Indeed, the water I give them will become in them a spring of water welling up to eternal life." The woman said to him, "Sir, give me this water so that I won't get thirsty and have to keep coming here to draw water." He told her, "Go, call your husband and come back." "I have no husband," she replied. Jesus said to her, "You are right when you say you have no husband. The fact is, you have had five husbands, and the man you now have is not your husband. What you have just said is quite true." "Sir," the woman said, "I can see that you are a prophet. Our ancestors worshiped on this mountain, but you Jews claim that the place where we must worship is in Jerusalem." "Woman," Jesus replied, "believe me, a time is coming when you will worship the Father neither on this mountain nor in Jerusalem. You Samaritans worship what you do not know; we worship what we do know, for salvation is from the Jews. Yet a time is coming and has now come when the true worshipers will worship the Father in the Spirit and in truth, for they are the kind of worshipers the Father seeks. God is spirit, and his worshipers must worship in the Spirit and in truth." The woman said, "I know that Messiah" (called Christ) "is coming. When he comes, he will explain everything to us." Then Jesus declared, "I, the one speaking to you—I am he." John 4:1-26

In this story of the woman at the well, Jesus hears from the Holy Spirit and discerns that this woman has had five husbands. He doesn't judge her, in fact, Jesus chose this woman to be the first person to whom He revealed that He is the Messiah! It was amazing that Jesus was speaking to her at all because she was a woman, by herself, and she was also a Samaritan. But the Father was pleased to have Jesus reveal Himself to her. If Jesus had not had this supernatural knowledge of her background, what He was revealing to her regarding Him being the Messiah would not have had the impact. After this encounter, we see that the woman is so touched by Jesus knowing this about her that she immediately rushes back to tell everyone in her town.

Then, leaving her water jar, the woman went back to the town and said to the people, "Come, see a man who told me everything I ever did. Could this be the Messiah?" They came out of the town and made their way toward him.
John 4:28-30

Having discernment for words of knowledge is a practical way to touch people's hearts and show them the love of our Messiah and King. These are spiritual gifts that are available to everyone! One day, God told me that a particular woman had severe back pain and that He wanted to heal her. I didn't know her very well, but her son was coming over to play with my son after school. When she called that afternoon to check in, I didn't sense (discern) that it was the right time to share, but when she came to pick him up, I sensed that the timing was right. I asked her, "You don't happen to have pain *right here* on your back, do you?" I pointed on my back to the spot that God had told me. She looked at me in shock, with wide eyes and said, "Well yes, I do! It hurts really badly right now. How did you know?" I told her that God told me and that He loved her and wanted me to pray for her so He would heal her back. She agreed to the prayer, and then got up and was walking down the stairs talking to herself, "This is crazy, I can't believe this, how would she know that, I can't believe the pain is gone…" She kept poking around on her back to try and find the pain but it was gone! That was the weirdest thing that had ever happen to her! Praise God her back was healed, her pain was gone, and she started being more active.

Discerning God's Holy Angels

Praise the Lord, you his angels, you mighty ones who do his bidding, who obey his word. Psalm 103:20

There are holy angels in heaven that obey God and serve Him only. Their purpose is to carry out God's will on earth. They harken unto God's Word, so proclaim His Word boldly and release them to work for God! Each person has at least two angels assigned to them from birth, and their purpose is to help you fulfill God's purpose in your life. In the book of Matthew, we see that even children have "angels," *plural*, meaning, *at least* two.

"See that you do not despise one of these little ones. For I tell you that their angels in heaven always see the face of my Father in heaven." Matthew 18:10

There are many types of angels: angels that guard the throne, warrior angels, worship angels, healing angels, provisionary angels, guardian angels, and more. Some deliver messages from God to us, and others deliver our prayers to the Father. We are not supposed to pray to or worship them; God alone is worthy of this honor. We can, however, receive messages from God through them, so being able to discern their presence is of utmost importance. We can talk to them, just like Abraham, Sarah, Joshua, Moses, Daniel, and Mary did in the Bible. Even more than we are aware of demonic spirits, we should cultivate discernment for God's Holy Angels. God's angels are much more powerful than demonic angels, and God has given us these *helpers* to fight spiritual battles for us.

An "angel" simply means "messenger". Some angels are messengers for God and others are messengers of Satan. We

An "angel" simply means "messenger". Some angels are messengers for God and others are messengers of Satan.

40

need to have discernment by the Holy Spirit to know which is which. Sometimes God's holy angels can be terrifying, and sometimes Satan's angels come disguised as angels of light. God wants a people that are mature and discerning so that we are aligned with heaven and working with God's holy angels!

We cannot expect to fight spiritual battles on our own. Christ has seated us in heavenly places so that we may reign with Him and bring heaven to earth. I wondered deeply about what it meant to reign with Christ in heavenly places. Who does God reign over? God reigns over His holy angels and His people! Since we are God's people, we don't reign over each other, and that only leaves one group left: the holy angels. Because Christ lives in us, we can pray for God to release His holy angels to help us. This may sound strange to you, but God has confirmed this to me time and time again. There are a lot of teachings right now coming out about this topic. There is also a lot of false teaching too, so be careful and always confirm everything with God yourself. If we end up prideful and dominating, then we are no better than Satan. God's angels are here to help us carry out God's will on earth. We don't reign over them so we can get a bunch of things for ourselves, but rather, so we may help others and share the good news of the Gospel!

In order to work successfully with God's holy angels, we need to have the fear of the Lord. Those aren't our angels, but are there to serve God and those that God has chosen to release His will into the earth through prayer. We know that when we fear the Lord, He sends His angels to camp around us.

The angel of the Lord encamps around those who fear him, and he delivers them. Psalm 34:7

God's angels also protect us and keep us safe. We can read thousands of testimonials of people that have had angelic encounters like this. If they are guardian angels, they're purpose is to keep us alive. When I had my first angelic visitation, God showed me that He had saved my life on numerous occasions, and He brought them all to my mind. He wanted me to be kept alive because I had a job to do for Him. He predestined me to do it. Although the enemy attempted to take me out numerous times, God saved me!

For he will command his angels concerning you to guard you in all your ways. Psalm 91:11

The Lord Jesus is our High Priest, and He calls His people a holy nation and a royal priesthood. We were chosen by God to walk into the light of the Kingdom of God. In God's Kingdom of Light, we are His people and He desires for us to let Him work through us to bring His Kingdom of Light to the earth. He wants us to declare His Word on the earth! When we declare God's Word, we release God's angels to work. We are God's chosen vessels to bring peace and joy to the earth!

But you are a chosen people, a royal priesthood, a holy nation, God's special possession, that you may declare the praises of him who called you out of darkness into his wonderful light. 1 Peter 2:9

Because we are "in Christ", we have many blessings that we probably have barely realized. We are a new race of man, under a new covenant, and for those of us who perceive and understand, we are given the keys to the Kingdom of God.

"I will give you the keys of the kingdom of heaven; whatever you bind on earth will be bound in heaven, and whatever you loose on earth will be loosed in heaven." Matthew 16:19

Ministering Spirits

God sends angels to deliver messages for Him and to proclaim His will for our lives. We see this in the story of the virgin Mary, when the angel tells Mary that she will bear a son, and He will be the Son of God. Notice how Mary agrees to God's word sent by the angel and says, "May your word to me be fulfilled." Mary could have said, "No thanks!" God sent this angel to deliver the message of His will to Mary. Sometimes the plans God has for us are so awesome that we need to have an experience like this for us to get on board.

"I am the Lord's servant," Mary answered. "May your word to me be fulfilled." Then the angel left her.
Luke 1:30

In the next story, we see a vision of what happens to Joshua when He encounters an angel of the Lord. Even though this man is a High Priest, he still has filthy rags before God, just like us. This is a picture of what it is like for believers when we repent of our sins before God. He removes our filthy clothes, washes us with His word so that we can walk in obedience to Him, and then He gives us a place of honor to govern His house!

Then he showed me Joshua the high priest standing before the angel of the Lord, and Satan standing at his right side to accuse him. The Lord said to Satan, "The Lord rebuke you, Satan! The Lord, who has chosen Jerusalem, rebuke you! Is not this man a burning stick snatched from the fire?" Now Joshua was dressed in filthy clothes as he stood before the angel. The angel said to those who were standing before him, "Take off his filthy clothes." Then he said to Joshua, "See, I have taken away your sin, and I will put fine garments on

43

you." Then I said, "Put a clean turban on his head." So they put a clean turban on his head and clothed him, while the angel of the Lord stood by. The angel of the Lord gave this charge to Joshua: "This is what the Lord Almighty says: 'If you will walk in obedience to me and keep my requirements, then you will govern my house and have charge of my courts, and I will give you a place among these standing here.
Zechariah 3:1-7

The house of the Lord is full of angels, those heavenly hosts who praise Him and do His bidding forever! God sends angels to deliver us, save us, help us, feed us, warn us, guide us, comfort us, and more. Although there is so much false worship in this area, we cannot ignore this part of God's Kingdom. I cannot tell you enough how we are not to worship or pray directly to these beings. They would be disobeying God's orders if they accepted your worship or offerings. These beings are not God, but rather, they serve Him, just like we do. They are spirits so they can move in the spiritual realm and deliver messages to people according to God's will. We need to let the Holy Spirit direct us on what to pray for and also have discernment of what messages we are receiving.

God sends angels to deliver us, save us, help us, feed us, warn us, guide us, comfort us, and more.

Angels in the Bible

Here is a collection of Scriptures I selected that show how God used His Holy Angels to deliver messages to His people and help carry out His will on earth. As you will see, God's angels are

His faithful messages that help His people carry out His will. God's angels still help His people today, and, with understanding, you can learn to work with them as well.

Genesis 16:10 – Angel tells Abraham that he will multiply his descendants.

Genesis 19:15 – Two angels warn Lot to flee the city before they destroyed it.

Genesis 24:40 – An angel is sent ahead of Isaac to find a wife for him.

Genesis 28:12 – Jacob has a vision of the angels ascending and descending from heaven.

Exodus 23:20 – An angel is sent ahead of the Israelites to prepare the way for them to enter the Promised Land.

Numbers 22:22 – An angel is sent to oppose Balaam and stop him from cursing the Israelites who are blessed by God.

Numbers 22:31 – An angel opens Balaam's eyes so that he can see into the angelic realm temporarily.

Judges 6:12 – An angel is sent to encourage Gideon before battle.

Judges 13:16 – An angel refuses to eat a food offering, but tells them to offer it to the Lord instead.

2 Samuel 14:20 – An angel of the Lord is attributed to knowing what is going on in the land.

Job 1:6 – Angels present themselves before the Lord.

Zechariah 1:14 – An angel tells Zechariah to proclaim a word from the Lord to the people.

Luke 2:13-14 – A great company of angels come and praise God at the birth of Jesus.

Matthew 2:13 – An angel tells Joseph to take Mary and baby Jesus to Egypt for protection from Herod.

Matthew 4:11 – Angels attend to Jesus is the wilderness and strengthen Him.

Matthew 13:39 – Angels are called the "harvesters" at the end of the age.

Matthew 13:49 – Angels separate the wicked from the righteous.

Matthew 18:10 – Children are said to have angels in heaven.

Acts 5:19 – Angels opened the doors of the prison to let the apostles out.

Luke 12:8 – Jesus says that if we acknowledge Him before others, He will acknowledge us before the angels of God.

Matthew 26:53 – Jesus tells the disciples that He can call on His Father to release legions of angels to help Him.

Matthew 28:5 – Angels appear at the tomb and tell Mary the Savior has risen from death.

Matthew 22:30 – At the resurrection, people will become like the angels in heaven.

Hebrews 1:4 – Jesus is superior to the angels because of the name that God has given to Him.

Hebrews 1:6 – Jesus is God's first-born, and the angels of God worship Him.

Are not all angels ministering spirits sent to serve those who will inherit salvation? Hebrews 1:14

As we can see, throughout the entire Bible, angels are present and active in the lives of God's people. There are even more stories than this, but I've listed just a few to give you a little different perspective on angels. Angels work to bring about the fulfillment of God's will on the earth and to minister to those who will inherit salvation. Jesus was the first-born Son of God, and as believers, we enter into God's Kingdom as Sons and Daughters of God. We each are chosen for a specific purpose,

Angels work to bring about the fulfillment of God's will on the earth and to minister to those who will inherit salvation.

and we all have angels that attend to us because of who we have become as followers of Jesus. If we want to know how to work with them, all we need to do is press into God and cultivate our discerning heart by asking for the Holy Spirit to guide us in all things. When we turn to God for the answers we seek, He rewards us with solutions that are too great to describe! Some of us may see into the angelic realm, and some of us may simply sense their presence.

Either way, whatever purpose God has for you, you can be sure that His angels are co-laboring with you to help you succeed! Pray now for God to give you a discerning heart and to open your spiritual eyes!

Prayer for a Discerning Heart and Spiritual Sight

ABBA Father, Thank You for Your Son, Jesus, who washed away my sin. Thank you for purifying my spirit and making me a new creation! Please remove this heart of stone, and give me a heart of flesh that hears Your voice. Remove the scales from my eyes so that I may see the beauty and Truth of Your precious Word. Help me to realize the splendor and majesty of who You are. Open my eyes and increase my awareness in knowing when Your angels are working on my behalf. In Jesus Name I pray, Amen.

CHAPTER 3

A Defeated Enemy

The key to defeating our enemy is realizing that Jesus already defeated him. We are new creations in Christ, and we need to share the love and victory of Jesus!

Understanding how the enemy operates in people's lives will help you overcome him yourself and will help you walk with God and live under the Father's blessings.

When we really understand how God rules, we should never want to go against Him. He gave us a law to obey and expects us to walk according to His precepts. His ways are perfect, and His ruling is just!

He is the Rock, his works are perfect, and all his ways are just. A faithful God who does no wrong, upright and just is he. Deuteronomy 32:4

When we stray from God's commands, hold unforgiveness, or do not repent, we are not under God's protection. Being obedient to God and following Jesus will keep us safe. We must always be humble to God and watchful because even the best of us can fall. Lucifer was the most beautiful of all the angels God created, and he fell because of his pride. This is what God said about him:

"'You were the seal of perfection, full of wisdom and perfect in beauty. You were in Eden, the garden of God; every

precious stone adorned you: carnelian, chrysolite and emerald, topaz, onyx and jasper, lapis lazuli, turquoise and beryl. Your settings and mountings were made of gold; on the day you were created they were prepared. You were anointed as a guardian cherub, for so I ordained you. You were on the holy mount of God; you walked among the fiery stones. You were blameless in your ways from the day you were created till wickedness was found in you.
Ezekiel 28:13-15

The reason Lucifer was kicked out of heaven was because he wanted to be worshipped above God. He didn't want to obey God, so he rebelled and took one-third of the angels with him. There was mutiny in heaven. After the fall, Lucifer's name was changed to Satan, meaning, "to obstruct or oppose". In this case, it means to oppose God, to obstruct the path that leads to righteousness, and to oppose the children of God. In Hebrew, the name "Satan" means, "adversary". Satan is constantly accusing the sons and daughters of God of their sin, just as he was accused by God for his sin.

Since Satan and his followers were angels, God did not offer them forgiveness, but allowed them to live on the earth until they face their judgment. Satan and the angels that followed him are jealous of us because God offers salvation to man but not to them. This is why Satan wages war against us and is constantly accusing us before God. Satan is constantly trying to get us to sin and be disobedient to God. When we are repentant of our sins, God sees us just like He sees Jesus: clean, washed and righteous.

Sin means to "miss the mark," meaning that God has a way and an order and anything that doesn't align perfectly is considered sin. He gave us the Torah- the first five books of the Bible- which tell us how to live. All the blessings of the Father are listed and the curses that will come upon us for disobedience are listed as well. No one with free will can ever follow these laws exactly, which is why God planned redemption from the very beginning. The purpose of redemption is so that God can bring His people to Himself in order to have a personal relationship with them. Without a Messiah, none of us could ever be close to God because we all sin and fall short of the glory of God.

The Copy Cat Strategy

God wants us to renew our minds in His Truth and put on the mind of Christ; Satan wants to reproduce his demonic thought process in us so that we will think like him. Satan mimics God and all that He does and has successfully introduced a myriad of false gods and false prophets to the world that people follow and worship. These demi-gods are introduced and distract people from ever knowing the one true God. These demi-gods aren't the Creator of all things, they are *creations*. They are fallen angels that rebelled with Satan. Worshipping them will always result in blood. God the Creator already shed His own blood for us, so no more blood is necessary!

> *Be careful, or you will be enticed to turn away and worship other gods and bow down to them.*
> *Deuteronomy 11:16*

The fallen angels are referred to in the Bible as "demons". They are spiritual beings without a body. Demon, in Greek, is the word *daemon* which means, "fallen ones". There are many ranks in the spiritual realm and differing levels of power and authority.

For our struggle is not against flesh and blood, but against the rulers, against the authorities, against the powers of this dark world and against the spiritual forces of evil in the heavenly realms. Ephesians 6:12

When we are aligned with heaven, we live from a *heavenly* perspective of our life on earth. If we aren't aligned, we live from an *earthly* perspective on our way to heaven. We do not struggle against people, but we love people because God loves people. We are supposed to stand against the powers of the demonic realm, and bring the light of the heavenly realm to earth.

Godly Wisdom

When we follow God, we receive heavenly wisdom and supernatural gifts of the Holy Spirit. I probably can't convince you through a book; it is something you need to experience for yourself. No one can argue with your experience. We've got to have God's Holy Spirit for any of this to really register! When we aren't filled with the Holy Spirit, we are considered "wicked". The definition of wickedness, according to the Bible, is that we go our own way instead of going God's way.

There is a wisdom that comes from the world, and then there is true wisdom which comes from God. Eve ate the fruit from the forbidden tree because she thought it would give her wisdom.

When the woman saw that the fruit of the tree was good for food and pleasing to the eye, and also desirable for gaining wisdom, she took some and ate it. She also gave some to her husband, who was with her, and he ate it. Genesis 3:6

But does that mean God doesn't want us to be wise? Certainly not! He is the source of true wisdom which leads to life, and the wisdom of the world leads to death. God wants us to be wise of Him and His ways, and He will give us true wisdom.

I went through this myself in the beginning of my conversion. As I began to read the Bible, I realized that none of my wisdom compared to God's wisdom. I realized that I was utterly foolish and totally wisdom-less. "God, give me wisdom!" I exclaimed, and so He did. God also gave me the wisdom to realize that His people are perishing because they lack knowledge.

My people are destroyed from lack of knowledge.
Hosea 4:6

That was the beginning of an incredible unfolding of truths and revelations by the Spirit of Wisdom that explained all these things to me.

If any of you lacks wisdom, you should ask God, who gives generously to all without finding fault, and it will be given to you. James 1:5

God can give not only spiritual wisdom, but all kinds of wisdom. Some of the greatest minds in human history were given their wisdom by God. In fact, the richest king ever in the history of the world was known for having incredible wisdom. King Solomon prayed to receive a discerning heart so that he could rule wisely. God was so pleased with this prayer and that Solomon had not asked for riches or honor, that God decided to give him those things in addition to a discerning heart! (1 Kings 3:5-15)

King Solomon was greater in riches and wisdom than all the other kings of the earth. 1 Kings 10:23

God is the giver of incredible knowledge, and He will bless us with riches, glory, and honor when our heart is in the right place. Solomon sought wisdom in order to help others and live rightly before God. All things in this world were created by God and are owned by Him. God created a universe that hangs in a delicate balance that only He controls. God created all these things which eventually point right back to Him. Many top scientists including William Turner (founder of English botany), Francis Bacon (originator of the scientific method), Antoine Lavoisier (father of modern chemistry), Francis Collins (leader in genetics), Galileo (one of the greatest physicists, astronomers, and inventors that ever lived), and Isaac Newton (developer of the theories of gravity and planetary motion) all had faith in God. The more one studies the cosmos, or genetics, or anatomy, or light, or quantum physics, the more one realizes that there has to be an amazingly gifted and intelligent Creator.

How Demons Can Effect Our Lives

The thief comes only to steal and kill and destroy; I have come that they may have life, and have it to the full. John 10:10

Demons try to prevent us from receiving God's wisdom. When we sin, we open the door to let demons into our life. Through faith in Jesus, we have forgiveness of sin, and these creatures have no place in our lives. When we repent and turn to

God, we are freed from our oppressors, but sometimes, although defeated, they do not leave quietly.

If we confess our sins, he is faithful and just and will forgive us our sins and purify us from all unrighteousness. 1 John 1:9

All persons, whether saved or unsaved are affected by demons. We remove the "legal grounds" the demons believe gives them the right to stay by having faith in Jesus who took our place for the punishment of our sins. We must always be watchful and cautious because they wait for us to have a moment of weakness and then try to come into our lives. God gives us authority over these creatures. They are like pests that need to be told, "Get!" God already did the work to remove their right to torment us, but we need to exercise our rights.

I had a dream as I was writing this book of me overcoming a demon that has been trying to torment me by messing with my son and our two little dogs. It has been trying to make me fear for their safety and keep my focus off of the book. In my dream, the demon had the shape of a huge brown dog, but it also had a strange appearance so I knew it wasn't an ordinary animal. First, I was outside with my dogs and it chased me inside, breaking down the door. An inner door protected me but I wasn't sure how long it would hold. As I began to close all other entrances to the house, there was a huge glass door which began to open because I had accidentally pushed a button to open the door instead of lock it. There were many other people and children in the room seeking shelter in my house from the animal. As the door opened, the animal lunged inside and grabbed my son's pant leg and was trying to drag him outside. I jumped right in between and told the animal to "Get out! Let go, in the Name of Jesus!" As soon as I made the command, the animal immediately let go and pranced away. When I woke up, I asked for God to show me the meaning of the dream, and He showed me that I had defeated a demon.

God was just showing me what was going on in the spiritual realm of my life. I didn't have any power to get that animal off my little boy, but the words I spoke were backed by the power of God Almighty and that was the authority it had to obey. The next day, all my strength returned, and I was no longer in a fog. The fear and worry was gone and I knew I had overcome by the power of Jesus!

Characteristics of Demons

The following is a list of the characteristics of demons which I have provided to help you to recognize when demonic activity might be present. To properly diagnose your situation, however, you need the Holy Spirit to discern if in fact there are impure spirits. If you read this without discerning your situation through the Spirit, you could think you have a demon when that's really not the case.

Entice – Demons entice people to do ungodly things. They tempt you to do things for pleasure and try to justify the behavior by having you compare yourself others and say, "I'm not as and as so-and-so." They can also entice you into selfish behaviors that seem good on the surface but are really taking you away from more important things. Demons especially entice people with false religions and beliefs that they will be admired and respected because of their belief. This could also be within social groups and organizations that do "good" but promote alternate agendas which are contrary to God's Word.

Harass – They study you and are on your "tail." They wait until you are fed up and then jump in to harass you. This often manifests as outbursts of anger, frustration, and anxiety. Over time, this can lead to depression because you don't feel like doing anything in hopes that you'll avoid the harassment. You just don't want to deal with anything anymore, and you start to feel confined.

Torment – Review Matthew 18 and the tormentors. Unforgiveness makes you a target for torment. It often manifests physically in arthritis and torturing pain that can be crippling and binding. It may make you fear that you are going insane. It could also be spiritual torment, making you feel like you are guilty of unforgivable sin. Demons can also cause you so much torment that you begin to torment others.

Compel – They will compel you to seek joy in compulsive smoking, eating disorders, drugs and alcohol, excessive talking, shopping addictions, watching TV, or religious rituals.

Enslave – They especially enslave in the areas of sexual immorality and pornography, but it can be with anything. You may have a problem with this kind of demon if, even after repenting, you still commit the sin and then hate it and hate yourself. You say, "Never again!" and yet it still happens. Often, demons of masturbation manifest in the fingers, and will cause them to tingle and shake. Their purpose is to enslave you and cause you to feel guilt and shame so you will never realize who God made you to be.

Defile – They can try to make you feel dirty and unclean, causing you to spend excessive time bathing and grooming yourself. They defile your thoughts and make you believe you are ugly and repulsive. They will try to get you to defile your thoughts by getting you to watch ungodly shows, listening to ungodly music, and surrounding yourself with ungodly people. They constantly chip away at you and try to make you think you aren't worthy of God's mercy. They manifest especially when you worship or read the Bible. It could make you feel like you need to sleep whenever you try to pray, read, or worship. They have no problem with you staying up late to watch ungodly television shows, but try to read your Bible and you will get sleepy.

Doubt – They make you doubt God's word, or your value. They can cause you to doubt yourself, making it hard to make decisions. They whisper doubts in your mind all the time about everything making you worry. They will try to get you to doubt that God's way is the best way for you. They will try to get you to blame God for the bad things that happen in your life. Doubt is the opposite of faith.

Distract – They distract you from spending time fellowshipping with God, targeting children especially and causing illness to keep your focus away from God. They want to get you believe you don't have time for God, and that you have more "important" things to do. They will distract you with problems whenever you try to fellowship with other believers or volunteer in ministry. Often these distractions are car problems, colds and flu, unexpected errands, calls from work, family or friends that are unnecessary.

Deceive – They can cause spiritual deception in leaders and congregations. These doors are opened by pride and fear. This type will blind your eyes to the truth of God, and will find fault with all things that have to do with God. They can also deceive believers into thinking they are saved when they are not, or try to make you think you're not saved when you are. They can deceive you with pagan holidays whose histories are unknown which blaspheme God and worship false gods. They can deceive people into thinking the supernatural workings of God are from the devil. They can cause you to be resistant to the truth of God's Word and cause people to "cherry pick" the Bible rather then have a true intimate relationship with God.

Weaken/Kill – They will make you sick, tired, and even try to kill you or try to get you to kill someone else (or yourself). This can be any type of illness, particularly cancer, organ failures, strokes, seizures, and blood diseases. Any thought with a negative, condemning, insulting, or dominating voice is a demon that is trying to break you down. They want you to feel defeated and hopeless.

Pain and Accidents – They will cause you to fall, stumble, and hurt yourself "accidentally". They attack frequently, causing burns, broken bones, sprains, and cuts. They're purpose is to make you feel bad about yourself and prevent you from walking in faith. They will try and make you wonder why God allows these things to happen to you.

Restlessness – They can cause you to have insomnia and be restless. They often manifest as ADD, ADHD, and autism. They usually influence highly intelligent individuals and want to prevent them from using their gifts for God.

Don't be paranoid here, but don't be oblivious either. Just because a demon whispers thoughts into your mind doesn't mean you need to "cast it out". It might already be "out", it's just "trying to get in". It only can "come in'" if you open the door by agreeing to their lies and not standing firmly on the word of God. Focus your attention on God and not on the demon.

Submit yourselves, then, to God. Resist the devil, and he will flee from you. James 4:7

We are supposed to submit to God first so that we can be seated with Christ in heavenly places and receive the authority from God to overcome the enemy. Then we can resist the devil

58

and tell him to "Get!" He has to flee from us because God's authority backs up our words. We aren't supposed to pray to God to just remove them from our lives; we need to submit to God, and *then* resist the devil! If we don't resist him but simply hide and pray, God can't do anything. We need to stand up to the devil because Jesus commissioned us to do it.

If you believe in Jesus as your Savior then you have been given this authority whether you realize it or not. Receive your authority!

Jesus called his twelve disciples to him and gave them authority to drive out impure spirits and to heal every disease and sickness. Matthew 10:1

Jesus triumphed over Satan and his demons and exercised the authority given to Him by God to overcome them. We, too, like Jesus, are given this authority by faith, and through Him we have the ability to expand God's Kingdom and stomp the enemy. Let us ascend and rule with Christ in heavenly places! We are called to bring God's Kingdom to earth, and triumph as Jesus triumphed by the power of God in us. This victory is available to all believers.

"Whoever listens to you listens to me; whoever rejects you rejects me; but whoever rejects me rejects him who sent me." The seventy-two returned with joy and said, "Lord, even the demons submit to us in your name." He replied, "I saw Satan fall like lightning from heaven. I have given you authority to trample on snakes and scorpions and to overcome all the power of the enemy; nothing will harm you. However, do not rejoice that the spirits submit to you, but rejoice that your names are written in heaven." Luke 10:16-18

CHAPTER 4

Our Spiritual House

The Holy Spirit doesn't enter us without our permission, and God doesn't allow any other spirits to enter us without us giving them permission either. If we don't want them to bother us, we can exercise our authority and make them leave.

"Like a city whose walls are broken through is a person who lacks self-control." Proverbs 25:28

A person that doesn't control their spirit opens themselves up to being attacked by enemy forces. This verse is speaking of a siege against a city, and compares it to one's body, which is the living temple of God. The Holy Spirit will not dwell in an unclean vessel. Jesus cleans the vessel so that we may receive the Holy Spirit and glorify God the Father.

We need to maintain our boundaries and keep ourselves under control. That way, our walls may be secure, and we can serve the Lord fully, with all our hearts, strength, minds, and spirits. This, of course, is a refining process throughout our whole lives of joyfully submitting to God, repenting, asking for His Spirit to dwell in us, and demanding our victory over the enemy.

"Don't you know that you yourselves are God's temple and that God's Spirit dwells in your midst?"
1 Corinthians 3:16

We have good reason to control ourselves, and we have a "helper" to do so, the Holy Spirit. That doesn't mean we come to God after we've cleaned ourselves up. Jesus came to save sinners. That means that we are agreeing with God about our sin, repenting of it, and then living our lives from then on in dependence on the Holy Spirit to teach us how to follow God's Torah (Hebrew for "instructions"). It takes time to replace bad habits with good habits, so there are often backsliding and struggles. The mark of a true believer is a life that reflects a constant moving towards holiness and continued fellowship with God. We have proof of this because we will start to experience the fruits of the Spirit.

"But the fruit of the Spirit is love, joy, peace, forbearance, kindness, goodness, faithfulness, gentleness and self-control."
Galatians 5:22

There are many trials that we will go through in our walk with God. We are being conformed into His image. We can let God take residence in us and enjoy the fruit of His Spirit, also called, the Bread of His Presence.

Living this way is like making a loaf of bread. Many people don't bake their own bread today, but it's an excellent lesson in the life of a believer. First, you have to start with a field of dirt. All the stumps and rocks have to be removed, and the ground has to be ready for planting. Then, you need to plant your seeds. You water them next and wait for God to make them grow. Then you harvest the grain and beat it up (threshing), removing the grains from the rest of plant. Next, you grind it up into powder. Now you take the flour, mix it with water, and let it set for a few days until the yeast begins to eat the sugar in the grain and bubble. Then you take some of your start and add more water and flour, and a little salt. After that, you knead it and mix it until it's smooth. Then you let it rise and smack it down again, squishing down all the hot air pockets. After that, you shape the dough and let it rise again. Then the bread has to go through the heat of the oven to be baked to the *perfect goldeny perfection*. Finally, you can eat it. Jesus is the bread of life and went through that whole process, so He knows what it's like. It's for your best good that you go through it as well!

> *"Consider it pure joy, my brothers and sisters, whenever you face trials of many kinds, because you know that the testing of your faith produces perseverance. Let perseverance finish its work so that you may be mature and complete, not lacking anything." James 1:2-4*

People are not born perfect, but I'd like to eventually become that golden piece of bread. All the trials we go through can bring us closer to God and make us better or they can make us bitter. We need to experience *some* trials in order to produce the Fruit of the Spirit and the Bread of His Presence. We need the Holy Spirit to give us discernment whether we are going through a trial, or being attacked by the enemy.

The Battlefield of the Mind

The mind is the battlefield in which demons will try to confuse your thinking and draw you away from God. If they can corrupt your thinking, bad actions will follow. Every action begins first with a thought. Your brain controls what you do. What makes sense to us may not be the right thing to do. God's ways are higher than our ways.

"As the heavens are higher than the earth, so are my ways higher than your ways and my thoughts than your thoughts."
Isaiah 55:9

We cannot always trust our emotions and thoughts to lead us. We have to submit to God in all things, and let Him lead us. This is why the Bible tells us that the righteous will walk by faith. We cannot glorify God unless we walk according to His ways.

"However, as it is written: 'What no eye has seen, what no ear has heard, and what no human mind has conceived'— the things God has prepared for those who love him."
1 Corinthians 2:9

God has a plan for you, and the enemy wants to prevent that plan from ever unfolding. The enemy comes to steal, kill, and destroy, and it is our responsibility to submit ourselves to God and believe His word is true, even if we don't feel like it. I like to say, "Faith it till you make it!"

"For I know the plans I have for you," declares the Lord, "plans to prosper you and not to harm you, plans to give you hope and a future." Jeremiah 29:11

Demons will always make you doubt God and His goodness. They'll make you doubt and will try to intimidate you to not move forward in faith. Here are some ways demons can reside within us that prevent us from living our lives to the fullest measure that God has planned for us.

Emotions/Attitudes – Emotions are not singular. They are usually a bunch of emotions connected to a thought. Negative emotions travel in packs, so to speak. Rejection can lead to loneliness, loneliness to self-pity, self-pity to despair, despair to thoughts of death, thoughts of death to suicide. We are smart to keep our emotions under control and to immerse ourselves in God's Word and His love for us whenever things start to unravel within our minds. If we really get stuck, we may need help in being delivered from demons attached to these strong emotions.

All negative thoughts start from demons; they whisper to us in our moments of weakness, and eventually our thoughts begin to negatively affect our way of life. God always speaks kindly and full of love. He never pushes us into things, but always gives us a choice. God doesn't dominate or threaten us; He leads us lovingly like a shepherd leads his sheep. He also defends us like a shepherd defends his sheep, but we have to stay with the flock and follow Him – we can't wander off on our own. Sometimes we wander without realizing it, but sometimes we are just rebelling!

God always speaks kindly and full of love. He never pushes us into things, but always gives us a choice. God doesn't dominate or threaten us; He leads us lovingly like a shepherd leads his sheep.

Rebellion can cause a chain of events and emotions: rebellion to anger, anger to hatred, and hatred to violence. Sometimes the violence is with words and sometimes it is physical. Either way, we need to keep our mind on positive things and especially on the leading of the Holy Spirit.

The following Scripture has helped me tremendously over the years to keep my mind on heavenly thoughts. I like to repeat

64

this verse over and over, and it brings me much peace and joy whenever I get anxious.

"Rejoice in the Lord always. I will say it again: Rejoice! Let your gentleness be evident to all. The Lord is near. Do not be anxious about anything, but in every situation, by prayer and petition, with thanksgiving, present your requests to God. And the peace of God, which transcends all understanding, will guard your hearts and your minds in Christ Jesus. Finally, brothers and sisters, whatever is true, whatever is noble, whatever is right, whatever is pure, whatever is lovely, whatever is admirable—if anything is excellent or praiseworthy—think about such things."
Philippians 4:4-8

I had so many negative emotions prior to being saved, and demons tried to remind me of it constantly. At the moment I was saved, all the negativity left and I was filled with complete peace. But the demons wanted to keep me down and the people around me reminded me of my past. My negative emotions had defined me. I never realized it, but they did. When I was saved, I was transformed and went from being a dark shadow to a bright light. It freaked everyone out. It has taken years for many people in my family to accept the change. I am telling you this to encourage you because He wants to change you, too! Let God give you your identity, because being defined by other people will prove to be a snare.

"Fear of man will prove to be a snare, but whoever trusts in the Lord is kept safe." Proverbs 29:25

An attitude of unbelief doesn't glorify God. Through faith in God's Word we are restoring the glory of God and bringing

God's will into the world. It is not God's purpose to bring us to heaven one day and to have us suffer and live like hell until we get there. It is to His glory that we bring heaven to earth. "On earth, as it is in heaven…" Through faith, and not by doubt, we can bring God's will to earth. We can bring heaven to earth and dwell in His presence. Heaven is wonderful because the presence of God is there, and God's Spirit dwells in us! Jesus taught us a wonderful prayer. In the beginning He prays for God's will on earth, as it is in heaven. I believe that there is an open heaven over every believer and that we can bring the reality of heaven and God's truths to the earth.

"This, then, is how you should pray:
Our Father in heaven,
hallowed be your name,
your kingdom come,
your will be done,
on earth as it is in heaven.
Give us today our daily bread.
And forgive us our debts,
as we also have forgiven our debtors.
And lead us not into temptation,
but deliver us from the evil one."
Matthew 6:9-13

Tongue – Lying, criticism, gossip, exaggeration, blasphemy against God, unclean speech, negative talking, complaining, arguing - these things are not of God, and are not in line with His will. We are commanded to not let any unwholesome words come out of our mouth.

"Do not let any unwholesome talk come out of your mouths, but only what is helpful for building others up according to their needs, that it may benefit those who listen."
Ephesians 4:29

The psalms have much to say about the tongue as well, for example here:

"My tongue will proclaim your righteousness, your praises all day long." Psalm 35:28

We see that we are to proclaim God's goodness all day long. There is no room for bad speech. We have no reason, either, to boast among men, but should instead think of others as higher than ourselves. The tongue should only speak words that God has given us. What wisdom do we have that is not from Him? If we are falling into this pit frequently, we can pray for God to help us, but it is our responsibility to humble ourselves to God regarding our speech. God is sure to discipline us if we are claiming to be Christians and then not speaking in a way that glorifies Him!

It is wise to do what I like to call a "tongue audit" at the end of each day. It helps us to reflect on what we said, repent if needed, and then ask for God's guidance in this area. We are encouraged to be slow to speak. In other words, think about what we say before we say it. I think God intends for us to use His words in all situations and be in inward prayer at all times for what we say, especially in difficult situations. I can tell you from my own experience that this is what saved my marriage. Every time my husband and I were together, I would pray for the right words to say to him. Sometimes I hated what I needed to say because I felt like I had the right to be angry. But God showed me how to earn the respect of my spouse by speaking in love and with facts. Living by our emotions is like being tossed by the waves in a small boat - they are constantly up and down, going this way and that. I had to choose between listening to the demonic voices, or listening to the voice of God - kind of like the angel on one shoulder, and the little devil on the other shoulder!

Living by faith means listening and obeying God through faith that which is true according to His Word. We can restore impossible relationships by relying on the Holy Spirit to give us the right words. We do need to have courage, however, to speak them! We don't have to worry or rehearse and make ourselves crazy trying to figure out what to say or do. If we can just trust God, He will lead us through it. I would refuse to say a word to my husband unless I was prompted in my heart by God. I knew it was Him because it was all in line with the personality of God that is revealed through the Bible. I also knew it was the Lord because it was always based on truth, and it was always done in love.

Once I adopted this method, I was no longer offended by my husband or by others. It took a lot of humbling and forgetting about my ego for it to work. I thought for sure that I would be made out to be a fool and a doormat, but somehow quite the opposite happened. You see, since I stepped back and let God fight my battles, I was given

If we can just trust God, He will lead us through it.

peace about the situations. Yes, I had to say nice things when I certainly did not want to. And I had to confront people in a loving way, which was not in my comfort zone at all, as I would have much rather ignored the problem and hoped it went away!

But, alas, our problems don't just *go away*, they seem to follow us around until we have the courage to face them. I had to have faith that God is faithful to do what He says. I didn't totally trust Him at first, but He has never let me down. I agreed to follow His guidance on particular situations and after I saw positive results, I began doing this in all areas of my life. I believe it is impossible to keep the tongue in line with Scripture unless the Holy Spirit helps us. It is so easy to get caught up in emotions, or even influenced in not-so-noble conversations while in a group setting.

"The mouths of the righteous utter wisdom, and their tongues speak what is just." Psalm 37:30

As believers in Jesus Christ, we are called righteous before God. Not from our own works, but we put on Christ's righteousness. Imagine yourself perfected, with good speech, walking uprightly, helping Christ in His work to save a fallen humanity. This image of yourself, as a disciple and co-laborer with Christ will help you attain that righteousness. Whenever we need guidance in a particular area, we can refer to the old acronym, WWJD? (What Would Jesus Do?). He can relate to us in all things, as He also lived as a man and was tempted, insulted, betrayed, and abused. He is always available to us through the Holy Spirit, to counsel and comfort us when the world seems to be against us. And when we come to the Comforter, we are also coming to the Deliverer, and He can cleanse you if you will repent, and turn to Him to be lead.

Sex – God created sex, and it isn't an evil thing. It is a beautiful thing when conducted by a married couple. It represents God's relationship with us, the man (God) goes into the woman (human) via the Holy Spirit. The church (believers) is called the Bride of Christ. It is an intimate relationship of knowing one another. However, compulsive sexual behavior, fetishes, masturbation, feminism, lesbianism, incest, and homosexuality are all evil practices. They are always demonic. It doesn't mean the person is completely *possessed*, but rather in bondage to these types of behaviors, their minds being poisoned by perversion and corrupted by demonic influence.

Demons try to damage this structure of husband and wife together and make us believe that the "grass is greener".

Lusts – This can include perverted desires and appetites, gluttony and food obsessions, shopping and overspending, power and domination, and addictions (to any worldly thing).

"For everything in the world—the lust of the flesh, the lust of the eyes, and the pride of life—comes not from the Father but from the world." 1 John 2:16

In this verse, it explains exactly what the Bible means by "lust". Lust of the flesh is being overly concerned with things that have to do with the body, as in overeating or undereating, obsessing about your image, trying to seek physical pleasures, etc. We also learn from this verse that these things come from the world and are not of God.

Lust of the eyes can be anything that is visible that causes envy or obsession, as in overly decorating your home, being envious of your neighbor's/friend's possessions, or constantly needing to see more and more natural geographic beauty or traveling for the purpose of visual gratification.

Pride of life is referring to being prideful or arrogant about one's financial status, family line, accomplishments, etc. All these things lack humility, and distract us from the true riches and pleasure of heavenly gifts.

The Bible tells us that God wants us to have all the good things in the world and that we will lack nothing.

The lions may grow weak and hungry, but those who seek the Lord lack no good thing. Psalm 34:10

But we are also commanded to not "worry" about such things and go chasing after them like everyone else.

"Therefore I tell you, do not worry about your life, what you will eat or drink; or about your body, what you will wear. Is not life more than food, and the body more than clothes?"
Matthew 6:25

We are to be Kingdom-minded, seeking first the Kingdom of God, and God will give these things to us. Just like with King Solomon: he prayed for a discerning heart, and God gave it to Him along with the greatest riches and glory a man has ever seen.

But seek first his kingdom and his righteousness, and all these things will be given to you as well. Matthew 6:33

History of Occult Activity/Idolatry - You may be affected by your grandparents' or parents' involvement in occult activities, secret societies, or worship of idols. This manifests often as diseases or abnormalities passed to the child by the mother or father (for example: asthma, allergies, heart disease, diabetes, arthritis, depression, cancer, etc.)

Our own personal involvement in the occult is also an invitation to bad health. All these New Age practices are bringing sorrow upon people and they don't even know it. Whenever we do these things, it is sin, and we need to repent of it. If we don't, we are living under a curse from God, plus, we are entertaining demons and fallen angels. All the "spirits" that claim to help us become idols and separate us from true love and joy which comes from God alone. Any involvement, even casually, is an agreement to let demons into your life. The Bible explains occult activity:

"There shall not be found among you anyone who burns his son or his daughter as an offering, anyone who practices divination or tells fortunes or interprets omens, or a sorcerer or a charmer or a medium or a necromancer or one who inquires of the dead, for whoever does these things is an abomination to the Lord."
Deuteronomy 18:10-12

This also includes horoscopes and superstitions, or any objects in your house that glorify the devil or any fallen angel (idol/god, ex. Buddha's, dragons, fairies, wizards, etc.) Basically anything that does not glorify God you may want to evaluate and remove from your home because spirits can dwell within objects. Lucky charms and talismans are nothing more than demonically charged objects disguised as helpful tools. The only helpful tool we need is the Holy Spirit!

Occult practice is so widespread that even "devout" Christians are subject to fall into it if they are not watchful. If we don't know what we are doing is bad then the punishment is light, but for those of us who know and still do it, the punishment is harsh. Either way, we need to really hate sin and love the things of God, never making excuses for things we do, but constantly seeking to align ourselves with the will of God.

All False Religions – This includes any religion that denies that Jesus is the divine son of God, lived as a man, died, and was resurrected on the third day. Jesus is equal to the Father and to the Holy Spirit, and is the creator of everything that is created. There is one God, Who is eternal, and the only way to know Him is through receiving salvation through His son, Jesus. False religions include, but are not limited to: Islam, Jehovah's Witnesses, Catholicism, Buddhism, Mormonism, Hinduism, etc. There are also plenty of false doctrines and religious spirits that have infected mainstream Christian churches. I believe there are saved people that are members of all the churches listed above – I'm not saying any entire group is unsaved. I'm saying that if we truly follow Jesus, we will have major problems with the doctrines of these churches. There are even non-denominational Christian churches that say they believe God, but there is no faith behind their statements. We need to stop relying on other people to tell us what is true and find out directly from God! He desires to be our personal High Priest, and He would like to make us one of His Priests.

But you are a chosen people, a royal priesthood, a holy nation, God's special possession, that you may declare the praises of him who called you out of darkness into his wonderful light. 1 Peter 2:9

All Heresies - This has to do particularly within the Christian church, and refers to doctrines of man that have not been inspired by God, but are rather, as the Bible says, "doctrines of demons". These "doctrines" cause disunity within the body of Christ and cause people to deny their fellowship with God, while strengthening it temporarily with each other. I say temporarily because often times this causes people to create denominations, but some members will disagree, and then they will leave and start a new church with the doctrines they see as important.

All the heresies have a basis in man deciding what is important, instead of having Jesus as the head of their church and directing each decision. They are based on man's opinion of what is right and not on truth. Feelings are imbedded in our opinions, and things can get sidetracked very quickly. 1 Timothy has it summed up quite nicely:

"The Spirit clearly says that in later times some will abandon the faith and follow deceiving spirits and things taught by demons. Such teachings come through hypocritical liars, whose consciences have been seared as with a hot iron."
1 Timothy 4:1-2

The chapter goes on to explain how some religions will forbid marriage and advocate abstaining from certain foods, which God created to be received with thanksgiving. These heresies are fed by religious spirits that are trying to twist our understanding of the truth of God's word. These deceiving spirits also try to keep deliverance ministry, healing and prophecy out of the church.

Physical Bodies – Demonic spirits can also reside in our physical bodies and manifest as epilepsy, asthma, heart problems, cancer, and especially skin problems. Although our spirits may be connected with God in Spirit, our physical bodies are separate and are therefore vulnerable to demonic attachments if we are not exercising our authority over them.

But he was pierced for our transgressions, he was crushed for our iniquities; the punishment that brought us peace was on him, and by his wounds we are healed. Isaiah 53:5

Jesus suffered and took on the curses and punishments that we should have experienced. If we are experiencing pain and suffering, and we know we are bought and purchased by Christ, then we can stand against it in the Name of Jesus. We can tell cancer to "Go!" And we keep saying it until it becomes true. We have to *know* for sure that we are right. We can't *hope* that the spirit of cancer will leave; we need to make it go! We aren't supposed to exercise our authority in some other point in the future. Some people claim we need to wait until the millennium to do this. But in the millennium, Satan and his demons will be bound for a thousand years so we won't need to do it then! We are supposed to stomp hell right now and walk with our God as the victors we are made to be.

He seized the dragon, that ancient serpent, who is the devil, or Satan, and bound him for a thousand years.
Revelation 20:2

Domination/Manipulation – This is usually a dominating mother, or a man who has never "cut the cord" and is dependant on his mother emotionally or financially as an adult. Anyone who controls you by guilt, shame, or anger is causing a dominating relationship. If you grew up around someone like this, you may need to distance yourself from them until you are spiritually strong enough to be around them for extended periods of time.

Sometimes we need time to mature and grow strong in our faith before engaging with these people for long periods. Short visits are sometimes okay, but in other cases it's just better to stay away from them and give ourselves time to heal. Otherwise, once we are delivered we could easily fall right back into it.

If you are in a marital relationship like this, you may need to separate yourself from your spouse for a while so that you can learn how to resist them in order to keep your deliverance. This can also apply to a woman who dominates her husband and does not respect his position, manhood, or authority. This is a common problem today, and although many times it seems that men should step-up and be better leaders, it is still not appropriate for women to dominate men - especially in marriage. This often leads to women treating their husbands like children and being disrespectful to them; eventually the marriage dissolves. If anything is demonic, this is, and it is ruining marriages everywhere.

Prenatal Influences - Unwanted pregnancies or resentment toward the child can affect the baby. Traumas during pregnancy or feelings of fear, rejection, instability financially or emotionally, or resentment towards the child can cause impure spirits to enter the mother and then also the child. We see in 1 Peter that women are called the children of Sarah and Abraham if we do not fear anything. Women are especially susceptible to fear. The spirit of fear is very strong and if it enters the woman during her pregnancy, it can be especially hard for the baby.

"As Sarah obeyed Abraham, calling him lord. And you are her children, if you do good and do not fear anything that is frightening." 1 Peter 3:6

Early Childhood Stress/Trauma - Most demons enter a person before the age of 5 years old. Children are especially vulnerable and depend on us for prayer and protection. We need to know how to pray for them and keep them from demonic attacks. Anger and unforgiveness are open doorways for demonic attachments. Disobedience to parents, lying, stealing, and even the strain of experiencing trauma or stress caused by poverty, divorce, abuse, or neglect can be signs that there are demonic attachments. Children that think they are unwanted are prime targets for a lifetime of torment.

Moment or Place of Weakness - This can be physical or emotional. For example, someone gets into a motor vehicle accident and suffers a head injury. The wound heals but during that moment of weakness a spirit of epilepsy enters. Whenever we are physically weak, we can be vulnerable to impure spirits. Often accidents can lead to resentment, anger, bitterness, self-pity, fear, anxiety, and unforgiveness - the pathways through which demon spirits can enter. We must be completely honest with ourselves on this issue; even small amounts of hatred or resentment can open us up to torment. These emotions can manifest into unhealed wounds and dominate your life. As children of God, we are expected to forgive others so that our Father in Heaven may forgive us.

"Do not judge, and you will not be judged. Do not condemn, and you will not be condemned. Forgive, and you will be forgiven. Luke 6:37

Sinful Acts or Habits - These can include, but are not limited to, drugs/alcohol, prescription medications, immoral sexual behavior, exposure to inappropriate language (television, music, etc.), theft (shoplifting), gossip, envy, overspending, selfish ambitions, and disrespecting authorities (especially parents). Confession and repentance are necessary for these types of demons to be removed. Fasting may also be required if habits involve food, drinks, or sugar, as your desire is caused by the impure spirit, and *feeding* the spirit what it wants will only make things worse. Sinful acts and habits can virtually be anything that does not honor the body (remember it is a temple of the Holy Spirit), or that is "un-Godly". Usually any good thing in excess can turn into a type of bondage - it takes control over you. Sinful acts are things that you refuse to give up easily and that are not led by the Holy Spirit.

Note on Deliverance:
When in doubt, cast it out. "In the Name of Jesus, I command you to go!" You will know when you are free because you will feel the peace of God. You may not feel free immediately, but you'll know in your spirit that you are. I have found that if people think there is something demonic going on, their intuition

When in doubt, cast it out. "In the Name of Jesus, I command you to go!"

is usually correct. Also, keep in mind, demons don't always manifest because they aren't connected to us strongly enough. There is a difference between *possession* and *oppression*. 99% of the time, we are simply being oppressed by believing their lies or because of witchcraft or curses. Most of these leave quietly. In more serious cases, their roots run deep, so you'll have to say it like you mean it: "In the Name of Jesus, Yeshua Hamashiach, I command you to come out, roots and all!"

Sometimes it takes time and prayer to identify the cause of how the demons entered, but sometimes it just isn't possible to know how the spirits entered, and that is okay. I don't encourage people to dig up their past and re-live horrible experiences. God knows what you went through; He's not the one reminding you of your past, it's the demons that are. I don't recommend visiting your past apart from the cleansing blood of Jesus. My purpose in explaining how demons enter is so that you can identify them and stand against them by the power of Christ in You. If you have been cursed because of witchcraft or occult activity, you'll need to renounce it and apply the blood of Jesus. The authority of Christ in the believer is enough to break every chain, every curse, and every stronghold. Witchcraft is one of the fastest growing practices in the world, and we can pray like this to protect ourselves:

Prayer for Protection from Witchcraft and Curses
Heavenly Father, In the Name of Jesus, I apply a bloodline of protection around (house, church, school, person, workplace, family, etc.). I lift and remove any curses spoken against them. Please send your angels to protect (house, church, school, person, workplace, family, etc.). Thank You, Jesus, Amen!

CHAPTER 5

How To Be Delivered

Jesus gives His followers authority over all sickness, disease, and demons. He has all the power and authority on the earth, and He has given this authority to the Body of Christ. It comes along with the whole package of salvation. We are called to go out and proclaim God's Kingdom *and* heal the sick.

And he sent them out to proclaim the kingdom of God and to heal the sick. Luke 9:2

The Holy Spirit will show you the steps needed to help people be freed from demons and healed. Not all sickness is caused by demons, but if it is, you'll discern it through the Holy Spirit. Jesus shows us in the Bible that we do not always need to talk with demons, we just need to tell them to go.

When evening came, many who were demon-possessed were brought to him, and he drove out the spirits with a word and healed all the sick. Matthew 8:16

I love those three words: WITH A WORD. With a word, Jesus drove out the spirits. With a word, Jesus healed ALL the sick. That's what the Bible says. Check it out. Read the entire chapter in context. Read all the examples if you need to. The authority piece is the part that is needed, and that is based on faith. Prayer and fasting may be needed to focus your energy and realize your authority. But, either way, if you really want to live free and help other people be free, Jesus and all the heavenly hosts will help you! Here a few guidelines that you can follow to make sure you are meeting the requirements to be delivered:

Be Humble – James 4:6 says "God opposes the proud, but gives grace to the humble." It is our job to humble ourselves. It would be inappropriate to pray for God to humble us; He commands us to "humble ourselves". Being humble is an attitude that we choose to have towards God and others. It is only when we come to Him humbly and without pride that He will show mercy to us.

> *"Humble yourselves before the Lord, and he will exalt you." James 4:10*

Be Honest – Do not act like you don't have a problem. Call it what it is. Look inward and evaluate your feelings. Ask God to show you anything that you are overlooking. If you are angry, anxious, depressed, overwhelmed, confused, or fatigued, call it that. You don't need to explain anything; just take responsibility for your feelings and decisions. This isn't about anyone else or what happened to you, it is how you have internalized and dealt with things. It is okay to feel like you are losing your dignity temporarily, God will give it back to you once the demonic spirits are gone. This is not the time to be prideful and sugarcoat your issues.

Confess Your Faith in Christ – Only the children of God have the "right" to be delivered. Verbally confessing your faith is essential in letting demons know that you are God's child, and that you are not in rebellion against God.

Confess all Known Sin – I also recommend repenting of all sins, whether you are aware of them or not! Pray for God to reveal to you any sin that you have left out. Sometimes it is necessary to repent of particular sins for particular types of demons. For example, there are demons that specifically relate to abortion. These demons often cause cancer and will not come out unless the person repents of the abortion and asks for mercy from God.

Repent of all Sin – Repenting of sin means that you agree with God that what you did was wrong, and that you are truly sorry. It also means that you recognize God and His authority, and want to come under His authority and headship. It is not just saying you are sorry. There is much more to true repentance than saying you are sorry. If you intend to sin again, God knows your heart and does not forgive you. You must come with a pure heart, and sometimes desperation is key- real passion. Sin is "missing the mark" and going your own way instead of God's way. Repenting means to turn back to God, to pitch your tent with Him. In return, God pitches His tent with you. If you don't want to pitch your tent in God's camp, then you really are just trying to avoid the consequence of your sin. The enemy has done a spectacular time keeping people in bondage by blinding them to true repentance. If someone comes to you to apologize, you know whether or not they mean it, and so does God.

Break all Ties with the Occult/Secret Societies – This means cleaning house. Objects can be homes to evil spirits, and any object that glorifies a false deity, demon, witch, or spirit can be bringing demonic influence in your home. All those Halloween decorations? Get them out! Ouija boards, tarot cards, angel cards (Yes, angel cards! God alone has supreme power, not angels.), Buddha statues, etc. Also, secret societies are often led spiritually by fallen angels, even when the group appears to do good deeds. You've got to break ties with these groups personally, and renounce associations with them by your parents or relatives.

Forgive Others – Jesus tells us to forgive others for their sins against us, so that our Father in Heaven can forgive us! We cannot walk in the light, free from anger, depression, anxiety, fear, and pain, if we are holding on to frustration or feeling like someone has wronged us. Forgiveness doesn't mean what was done is "okay", it just means that you aren't mad about it anymore. You are free to be happy. Demons love to remind you of things people have done to you so that you will hate that person. Un-forgiveness does nothing to make the wrong right; it just allows you to continue being hurt by it!

You can say something like this, "I forgive (Name) for what they did to me. I no longer hold it against them and I release all anger and resentment." That's it. Word it however you want. The point is letting it go. You can't be happy if you are mad about things that have happened in your past. You also have sinned against others, so who are you to hold something against someone else? No matter what happened, you can forgive it. Even if you have to force out the words, it will work. Forgiveness is a choice, not a feeling. You will be removing the "legal grounds" for demonic torment because by forgiving, you are ripping out the roots of fear and anger which has allowed them to stay.

Worshipping God after this is very beneficial. Letting go of anger, and creating an atmosphere of joy and worship to God is something demons can't stand. Turn on some good worship music and play it loud! Sing along. Listen to the song, "Forgiveness," by Matthew West, and cry along. Just do it. Don't let un-forgiveness hold you back another day.

Renounce Curses – Curses are bad things spoken against someone. God is the first person recorded in the Bible to curse anyone; however, God gave us the "counter curse" by supplying a Messiah who took on the curse for us. Blessings come from God for obedience and curses for disobedience. Curses were often used during wars in Biblical times.

In fact, people in today's day still hire medicine men, witches, and magicians to curse families or people who have wronged them. Curses can be spoken against you deliberately, or they may have been brought upon you by being involved with activities that were against God or in worship to another false god or deity. It could be something spoken under someone's breath, "They are going to break their neck!", and then they fall and break their neck. It could be brought upon by demons for sin or bad behavior. Either way, you can pray and renounce the curses, but occasionally it is necessary to renounce specifics. For example, sometimes during war, even centuries ago, a family could be cursed by another family and until the curse is reversed, it still exists. It's considered "black magic" but it does work. Voodoo, spells, and black magic are all effective ways to curse people. To reject this truth is ignorance.

Jesus also is recorded as cursing as in the fig tree in Mark 11. God cursed Satan, Adam, and Eve after their first sin; curses go back to the very beginning. Scripture tells us that Jesus took on the curse for us, so we are free from the curse on mankind by God.

As children of God, we have the right to be free from all curses. You can pray this, "I renounce the curse spoken against me by (Name) and I release myself from it, in Jesus's name, Amen." With some physical conditions, especially with arthritis, the sickness can not be healed until the curse is renounced. So take the time and consider this as a possibility. As ridiculous as this idea may sound to you, I promise you it will be worth the time! If you believe in God's blessings, you should likewise understand curses and know that they are very real.

Expel – Don't be passive here. This is the time to be bold and proclaim your freedom because you are a child of God through faith in Jesus Christ. Be specific, direct, and firm in your prayer. Take authority over the demons, and kick them out! You don't want them or what they offer you anymore! They are unwanted visitors, and you might have to add a little attitude. Don't pray for God to take them for you. He already sent His son to die for you so you could be free. You have to take the authority God already gave you to overcome. The blood of Jesus does nothing if it is not applied! APPLY it to your life.

You need to reclaim your body as an instrument for righteousness and renounce using it as an instrument of evil. We have all fallen short of the glory of God, and yet this does not prevent us from having authority over demons. Jesus gained authority over them in His work on the cross, and He gave this authority to us to use for ourselves and to help others. Don't just wait for someone to do it for you. Take initiative, align yourself with God, and believe His promises. He who called you is faithful.

Breathe – After the command, "COME OUT, IN JESUS'S NAME!" be quiet and breathe. Spirits often come out on your exhalation. This is one of the more pleasant ways they come out, so don't talk too much or they might get stuck in your throat. Other symptoms you might experience are cough, headache, confusion, pain, abdominal problems, stomach ache, nausea (sometimes even vomiting), weakness, crying, laughing, yelling, fatigue, or trouble breathing. Go ahead and let your body do what it needs to do, don't try to stop coughing because you may be preventing the demon from coming out. In extreme mental illness and sexual abuse cases, more severe symptoms can be present. If you have a particularly difficult case, you may need help from an experienced Christian who can help you. Most demons come out easily, but sometimes they can take several hours. Either way, just be patient and keep going, do not be fearful. Ask for the Holy Spirit to guide you on what to do next if you aren't sure. Worship is a great way to spend the next few minutes, so get that music ready to press play as soon as you are done praying! In fact, I would recommend playing Christian music all the time, immersing yourself in God's word and worship, making the best possible environment for God and the worst possible place for the enemy.

Why Some People Aren't Delivered

Some people are not delivered because they don't meet the conditions to be delivered. If they are not believers the demons have every right to be there and the demons know it. Deliverance can be performed on non-believers and is a main theme in the New Testament, but without the indwelling of the Holy Spirit the demons can come right back. This goes for Christians as well. You can be a believer and still have huge areas of your life which are not under God's authority. Any area of your life that is not under the dominion of the Holy Spirit is empty and therefore available to demonic spirits.

Christians who repent, but do not convert are not really Christians at all. There are three kinds of people in the world: believers, make-believers, and non-believers. Most Christians today I would categorize as make-believers. These are people who repent and get baptized in water, but they never receive the Holy Spirit and become a new creation. They think they are going to heaven, but are headed straight to hell! This person has not been converted to Christianity. Conversion means, "to be changed".

Paul addressed the make-believers in the Book of Acts in Chapter 19. We not only need to repent, but we also need to convert. We must be baptized by the Holy Spirit and *into* the Body of Christ. We must let our old life die and be raised with Christ in the resurrection of the newness of life that is given through the Holy Spirit. This is a Spirit which does not want to sin. Sure, we still make mistakes, but our being is now filled with a Spirit that is from heaven. It is heaven minded and sin does not rule over it.

So from now on we regard no one from a worldly point of view. Though we once regarded Christ in this way, we do so

no longer. Therefore, if anyone is in Christ, the new creation
has come: The old has gone, the new is here!
2 Corinthians 5:16-17

If we are truly born of God and filled with the Holy Spirit, we live by the Spirit and no longer live by the flesh. When we are dead to ourselves, God recognizes our repentance, recognizes our baptism, recognizes the Blood of His own Son which has been applied by faith, recognizes our predestination in Christ, and our names are written in the Book of Life. We have passed from death into life. We have not received our heavenly bodies yet but we yearn for them because our flesh is weak and contradicts the spirit that is within us!

"Watch and pray so that you will not fall into temptation.
The spirit is willing, but the flesh is weak."
Matthew 26:41

We can be tempted, just as Satan tempted Jesus in the wilderness. We can overcome because the Holy Spirit is in us and helps us. If we draw near to God when we are tempted and exercise our authority over the enemy, we will overcome temptation every time.

No temptation has overtaken you except what is common to
mankind. And God is faithful; he will not let you be tempted
beyond what you can bear. But when you are tempted, he
will also provide a way out so that you can endure it.
1 Corinthians 10:13

People remain in bondage to sin when they are unconverted and living by the flesh. For example, if you are not yielded to God with the choices you make sexually, you are

86

probably doing sexually immoral things which you are not willing to give up. If you are not yielded to God in the area of food and treatment of your body, you are probably taking prescription drugs, eating unhealthy foods, and or drinking alcohol or using recreational drugs which you don't want to give up.

If you are not yielded to God in any area, it is because you are rebelling against Him in that area. You cannot be totally free until you are spiritually living in Christ, in that you die completely to your old self, bury yourself, and rise as a new creation into the body of Christ through the power of the Holy Spirit.

10 Main Reasons People Aren't Delivered

1. **Lack of Repentance** – Without true repentance we cannot receive redemption. Many Christians today fall into sin and think God doesn't care or maybe that He doesn't notice. They don't take the time to find out what God's truth is because they really don't want to know. But the First Commandment is that we love our God with all our strength, heart, mind, and soul. If we are to love God, we need to know what needs repentance and what doesn't. We can't afford to guess. You will not be delivered from something that you are really not sorry about, or your failure to see that your perception of yourself as "not that bad" is still not good in the eyes of the Lord. Failure to repent most often results in one's inability to receive supernatural physical healing because we'll never realize the authority Jesus gives us over all sickness and disease.

2. **Lack of Desperation** – Laziness and an attitude of indifference can prevent one from being delivered. If you see that someone needs to be delivered, be careful bringing it to their attention. If they are not ready to receive their deliverance, it *might* be effective, but chances are, the demons will return and they will be worse off than when they started. You have got to depend on

the Holy Spirit's leading on this. There are plenty of people out there that are ready to receive, so spend your time with them first. Their desire to have complete freedom is crucial in their long-term success. In Jesus's ministry, the people came to Him and He delivered and healed them. Sometimes we have to wait for them, as hard as it is sometimes to see people suffer, we need to realize that Jesus is the Shepherd and we must follow Him, not step ahead. For example, I knew a woman who wanted to be delivered but had a fortune telling business. Until she was ready to give that up and find a new trade, she was not ready to receive deliverance.

3. **Wrong Motives** – James 4:3 says, "You ask and do not receive, because you ask wrongly, to spend it on your passions." Deliverance from demons that are affecting finances is particularly sticky if the person is not ready to honor God with their money. If a person is praying for God to help them pay off their credit card debt but doesn't change their spending habits, they will eventually end up in debt again. One must confess their sin, repent to God, receive forgiveness, and then turn their ways towards God. We cannot be double-minded. God will bless us abundantly if we have faith in Him. But we cannot try to manipulate God into giving us things. God gives so that we may be a blessing to others. As His children, God wants us to have the best of everything. This is so we may glorify Him. If it only glorifies us and our own lusts then it wouldn't be a blessing from God, but a curse. When we are living in God's perfect will and focus on God, we can speak our life into reality. Whatever we ask for in prayer, with faith, we shall receive. If we know we are His and we are in His will, we can walk on the water if we want to!

You may ask me for anything in my name, and I will do it.
John 14:14

4. **Self-Centeredness** – Many enjoy the attention they get for their problems and are too self-centered to be delivered. Often, in cases of physical disability, if they were healed, it would mean losing their financial assistance and they would be expected to go back to work. This thought is often frightening for some, especially if their infirmity has gone on for a long time. Their infirmity is their whole life. It's their identity. Maybe they have even learned to be more compassionate to others because of it, and they even think it was God's idea to afflict them in the first place.

Sometimes the only attention someone gets is because of their illness, and the thought of losing the attention is not worth losing the ailment. Or maybe there are just too many uncertainties about life for the afflicted person to be comfortable receiving healing. But, really, self-centeredness and the inability to see outside one's own needs is the ultimate anti-Christian behavior. Some need help seeing past themselves and to gain perspective on the needs of others and the will of God before they can receive their deliverance.

There is a wonderful story in the Bible where a man throws down his "beggars cloak" after He is healed by Jesus. This is equivalent today to a disability allotment that allowed him to ask for alms. This is an example of someone who showed humility and had faith in Jesus.

Then they came to Jericho. As Jesus and his disciples, together with a large crowd, were leaving the city, a blind man, Bartimaeus, was sitting by the roadside begging. When he heard that it was Jesus of Nazareth, he began to shout, "Jesus, Son of David, have mercy on me!"
Many rebuked him and told him to be quiet, but he shouted all the more, "Son of David, have mercy on me!" Jesus stopped and said, "Call him." So they called to the blind

man, "Cheer up! On your feet! He's calling you." Throwing
his cloak aside, he jumped to his feet and came to Jesus.
"What do you want me to do for you?" Jesus asked him. The
blind man said, "Rabbi, I want to see." "Go," said Jesus,
"your faith has healed you." Immediately he received his
sight and followed Jesus along the road. Mark 10:46-52

5. **Failure to Break Ties with the Occult** – This can be generational sin or personal involvement. This can also include failure to remove occult objects in the home which are embodied with demonic spirits. Sorcery is the act of imparting demonic spirits into objects or even places, and if these objects are in your home the spirits can influence the environment and create blocks for a person to receive lasting deliverance. Maybe it is a little Buddha statue, Halloween decorations, a Ouija board, good luck charms, tarot cards, dragon statues (or other figurines), or maybe books on horoscopes or astrology. All these things are detestable to God and are open doors for the enemy.

6. **Failure to Sever Dominating Relationships** – This can be particularly difficult mainly because these relationships are often our closest relatives. It may take months for a person to get in an environment where their contact is limited from this/these person(s), and, once they do, they will be able to receive their healing. It may even require a person to see a counselor or pastor to work through identifying unhealthy relationships. When the person is distanced, they can receive their healing, and then work to grow strong in their faith before engaging with his person again. It is never God's will for us to avoid people, especially our family, and hold on to negative feelings or even fear of certain people. But it is okay if a person is in an unhealthy relationship for that person to distance themselves temporarily (possibly even months or years), so that they are able to heal and eventually restore the

relationship. But remember, restoration is always possible if God is in the midst. Don't ever lose hope, and always be aware of God's leading.

7. **Under a Curse** – As we have learned, curses can come to us based on our bad choices, or we can inherit them from our parents. We can also curse ourselves accidentally by speaking negatively about ourselves. "I'm such an idiot!" "I'm so fat!" "I'm never going to find a job!" Guess what, saying these things are all you cursing yourself! We can speak life or we can speak death. Proverbs 18:21 tells us:

> *"Death and life are in the power of the tongue, and those who love it will eat its fruits."*

We must renounce generational curses, curses spoken against us, and curses we have spoken against ourselves. We must also confess and repent of any sin that may have caused us to be cursed by God; as Jesus himself paid the price for us, so we were bought at a price, let us glorify God with our tongue.

8. **Failure to Confess a Specific Sin** – You cannot hide anything from God, so don't try. God already knows what you did, and He loves you anyway. He will not be disappointed if you confess your sins to Him, in fact, quite the opposite; when we confess our sins God is faithful to forgive us.

> *If we confess our sins, he is faithful and just and will forgive us our sins and purify us from all unrighteousness. 1 John 1:9*

The sin of abortion is considered murder in God's eyes. Often times schizophrenia, depression, and suicide demons will enter after someone has had an abortion. This is also true with

91

any type of murder, whether it is intentional or unintentional, this can open the door to the enemy. Any major trauma, whether you endured it or if you inflicted harm to another can open the door. Many times people have admitted to these specific sins, and right after have received healing and deliverance. When you endure trauma, you can harbor feelings of bitterness, fear, and hatred, which are opening the door for the spirit of un-forgiveness. You have to own your feelings and forgive all who have sinned against you, just as your Father has forgiven you.

"But if you do not forgive others their trespasses, neither will your Father forgive your trespasses." Matthew 6:15

9. **Not Separated by Water Baptism** – Water baptism does not grant you salvation, for this is done in the heart and with the mouth by repentance and faith in Jesus.

"Whoever believes and is baptized will be saved, but whoever does not believe will be condemned." Mark 16:16

The Israelites were freed from Egypt but they were removed from Egypt and separated by the water. So must we also be freed and separated from our bondage by going through water. We must also take the step to separate ourselves from Egypt by committing our life to Christ, being baptized in the name of Jesus Christ. This is a work that proves our faith in God, and our outward expression of something that happened in the heart. If a person is not willing to be baptized (original Hebrew word means "to immerse") he or she may not be able to receive his or her deliverance until he or she is willing to take that step of obedience and demonstrate worship to God.

10. **Part of a Larger Battle** - What you stand for or groups you are affiliated could be hindering your ability to receive deliverance. Your decisions and/or leadership may be promoting ungodly values or immorality, causing demonic spirits to have dominion over certain parts of your life. When you are really fed up and ready to make some changes, take a step in God's direction, and watch how He blesses you. This can often be risky, and may put your reputation at risk, but whose favor and admiration do you value most, God's or man's? Be courageous and take steps towards doing what is right. It may mean losing some money or prestige, but God is able to bless you abundantly if you are faithful to Him. It may mean rocking a few boats, and things might get messy for a little while. But with patience and perseverance, God will guide you through, and you will receive your deliverance and healing.

Note on Deliverance:

In some cases, you will need someone who knows their authority in Christ very well to overcome a powerful demon that has deep roots. Demons can, in some cases, cause fear and even physical pain. If you feel like you need help, or experience labored breathing or get extremely angry reading this, you may be in tighter bondage that requires help from someone with experience. Do not be embarrassed! Please seek help as soon as possible.

COMPLETE DELIVERANCE PRAYER

I confess Jesus as my Lord and Savior. I believe that You love me, and that You paid the penalty for my sins by dying on the cross, that You, Jesus, were buried and that You were resurrected on the third day. I believe You intercede for me because of my faith in You, and that because I have faith in You, I am saved by grace, and not because I have earned it.

I confess faith in being an accepted child of God, and I thank You, Jesus, for Your sacrifice for me. I repent of all my sins (take a moment to reflect on your sins). I forgive ALL who have sinned against me. I forgive (name each person).

I renounce all occult activity by myself and/or family members (generational sin). Right now, I lay down pride, bitterness, rebellion, hatred, and all forms of selfishness. Thank You, Jesus, for redeeming me from any curses; I release them now.

As a loved child of God, I am now free, and I command all demons to come out now. You no longer have any right to this body, for I am now owned by God. Holy Spirit, I receive You now; come and fill me, equip me, and teach me. Help me to be an instrument of God's love, and conform me into Your perfect image. I welcome Your leadership and I give myself fully to You, Jesus, without reservation. All I have is Yours. Allow me to see, hear, and grow in my personal relationship with You, Jesus. Give me a fire that shines a bright light for You, and help me to keep the fire fed with pure spiritual food. Amen!

CHAPTER 6

Living Victoriously

To live in victory, you need to give yourself fully to the Lord. This means that you truly "put to death" living by the flesh (or carnal nature), and live anew in the Holy Spirit, and devote yourself to learning and following God's commands. Any areas of your life where Jesus does not reign, or you are not led by the Holy Spirit will create a vacuum, which is open to demonic spirits to take residence.

> *"When the unclean spirit has gone out of a person, it passes through waterless places seeking rest, and finding none it says, 'I will return to my house from which I came.' And when it comes, it finds the house swept and put in order. Then it goes and brings seven other spirits more evil than itself, and they enter and dwell there. And the last state of that person is worse than the first."*
> *Luke 11:24-26*

As we see in this passage, Jesus is explaining how an unclean spirit returns to a house (our bodies) in which it once dwelled, finding it cleaned up and put in order, which is all great and fine. However, the problem is that the house was unoccupied; nothing was preventing the spirit from entering. Without the Holy Spirit, any area of our lives, even as believers, is open to demonization. We cannot be fully *possessed* by a spirit because we are owned by God, but if we do not dedicate our *house,* or body, to God and let ourselves be filled with His Holy Spirit, we are open to being influenced, enticed, and could eventually end up in bondage to these spirits in certain areas of our life, depending on how much we go along with them.

It is our responsibility to be sober (which, Biblically speaking, means to be serious, sane, sound-minded, disciplined, discreet, et cetera) and strive toward living a life that is holy and dedicated to God. We are united with God in Spirit, but our physical bodies can be a target (and residence) of impure spirits, if we are not yielded to God and have given authority to the unclean spirits instead.

"For the Lord your God moves about in your camp to protect you and to deliver your enemies to you. Your camp must be holy, so that he will not see among you anything indecent and turn away from you."
Deuteronomy 23:14

Put on a Garment of Praise

Let us bother Satan with our steadfast faith and worship, more than he bothers us! Let us be so dedicated and connected with God that there is no room for the enemy to creep in. The truth is, the closer we are to God, the less the enemy can harm us. But the closer we get, the harder the enemy tries to pull us away. We need to be steadfast in our faith and know what God's Word says when times get hard. No matter what is going on, we can still praise God for his majesty and goodness. Even when it seems like God has all but abandoned us, and our true faith is exposed as lacking, through praise and worship, we can display our faith and trust in God, and He will always come to our aid. The results may take time for us to see, but as we pray and sing and pronounce our faith to God, the enemy has no choice but to flee. Fellowship with God automatically defeats the devil. Intimacy with God will lead you to help others do the same.

Put on the Full Armor of God

The picture the following verses paint are a wonderful lesson in the daily life of a Christian. There are days of rest of course, but if you think you only need to use a few of these items in your life, you are mistaken. A warrior never goes out with only some of his armor. If he is smart, he will always be ready for anything. Keep in mind, one of the best strategies the enemy has is the "element of surprise". If you are expecting your enemy, he will think twice about his attack. If you are unaware and oblivious to him, you are a sitting duck. So let us not be ignorant of his schemes, but be strong in the Lord and ready for battle anytime. Not that we need to go looking for a fight; a soldier always waits for his orders. And keep in mind, our battle is not with persons with physical bodies, but rather, against the spirit behind the offense.

"Finally, be strong in the Lord and in his mighty power. Put on the full armor of God, so that you can take your stand against the devil's schemes. For our struggle is not against flesh and blood, but against the rulers, against the authorities, against the powers of this dark world and against the spiritual forces of evil in the heavenly realms. Therefore put on the full armor of God, so that when the day of evil comes, you may be able to stand your ground, and after you have done everything, to stand. Stand firm then, with the belt of truth buckled around your waist, with the breastplate of righteousness in place, and with your feet fitted with the readiness that comes from the gospel of peace. In addition to all this, take up the shield

of faith, with which you can extinguish all the flaming arrows of the evil one. Take the helmet of salvation and the sword of the Spirit, which is the word of God. And pray in the Spirit on all occasions with all kinds of prayers and requests. With this in mind, be alert and always keep on praying for all the Lord's people."
Ephesians 6:10-18

1. **Belt of Truth** – The sword (Word of God) hangs on the belt, so without truth, God's Word can be twisted. This means praying for the spirit of truth, and dedicating your time to the study of God's Word. This also means believing God and not doubting Him.

2. **Breastplate of Righteousness** – This protects your heart which needs to be filled with God's love and acceptance. God dwells in our hearts so we must protect that place and not let it be hardened by the world.

3. **Shoes Bringing the Gospel of Peace** - This refers to you walking rightly, prepared to share your testimony and to seek peace in all situations.

4. **Shield of Faith** – This shield is huge, large enough for you to hide your body completely behind it! It prevents the arrows from the enemy and his minions from touching you. Having faith in God's Word, will for your life, and promises will protect you from believing the lies of the enemy.

5. **Helmet of Salvation** – This protects your mind from negative thoughts that lead to guilt and shame. Your salvation and forgiveness of sins helps you to walk with a clean conscience, full of joy and thankful to God.

6. **Sword of the Spirit** – This is the Living Word of God, and refers to the Scriptures/Holy Bible and also to

personal revelation of God speaking to you. God's Truth and Living Word cut down the lies of the enemy and destroy their effects. The Sword of the Spirit can be reciting and proclaiming Scripture, and applying it to your life.

7. **Prayer in the Holy Spirit** – Spiritual prayer is releasing God's Truth and will to make what is prayed for manifest. It can be you praying from promptings by the Spirit, or it can be you praying in the Spirit in spiritual tongues if you do not know what to pray. It can be binding the enemy from further harm, it can be asking God for light on a particular situation, and it can be asking for a vision. We are to pray for spiritual gifts, including prophecy, the gift of revelation, the gift of tongues and interpretation, words of knowledge, healing, and authority. Ask and you shall receive. Prayer is the only piece of "armor" that reaches all the way to heaven – even the sword only goes a few feet, but prayer has no limit and is powered by faith, love, and truth. Prayer is an offensive weapon, and can bring down the forces of the enemy even over cities and countries. When we pray, God hears us immediately, and sometimes the answer is *The Bible tells us to pray without ceasing.* already on its way, for God foresaw what you were going to pray and already had the answer coming! The Bible tells us to pray without ceasing. God wants communion with you all the time and anything you ask that is in God's perfect will, will happen! Jesus encourages you to have faith! God will do whatever you ask if it is His will! And His will is for you to prosper

spiritually, and to have health and honor. Jesus addresses discouragement of unanswered prayers:

He replied, "Because you have so little faith. Truly I tell you, if you have faith as small as a mustard seed, you can say to this mountain, 'Move from here to there,' and it will move. Nothing will be impossible for you."
Matthew 17:20

The first five articles of the full armor of God are defensive. The last two are offensive weapons. All are necessary at all times. Leave one out and you will get a warped result. In any situation, we must be completely dressed. If you don't have a firm grasp on one of these, or think that one isn't that important, you need to study them at length. They are critical to your success because with understanding, they allow you to be fully equipped to serve God and help others.

Live by God's Word

After Jesus was baptized in water, and before he started His ministry, He went into the wilderness for forty days, and was tempted by Satan. On the last day, when Jesus was weakest, is the day the devil came to tempt Him.

"Then Jesus was led by the Spirit into the wilderness to be tempted by the devil. After fasting forty days and forty nights, he was hungry. The tempter came to him and said, "If you are the Son of God, tell these stones to become bread." Jesus answered, "It is written: 'Man shall not live on bread alone, but on every word that comes from the mouth of God.'" Then the devil took him to the holy city and had him stand on the highest point of the temple. "If you are the Son of God," he

said, "throw yourself down. For it is written: "'He will command his angels concerning you, and they will lift you up in their hands, so that you will not strike your foot against a stone.'" Jesus answered him, "It is also written: 'Do not put the Lord your God to the test.'" Again, the devil took him to a very high mountain and showed him all the kingdoms of the world and their splendor. "All this I will give you," he said, "if you will bow down and worship me." Jesus said to him, "Away from me, Satan! For it is written: 'Worship the Lord your God, and serve him only.'" Then the devil left him, and angels came and attended him."
Matthew 4:1-11

Notice how the Holy Spirit led Jesus into the wilderness. Jesus didn't decide to do this on His own. He was being obedient to the leading of the Holy Spirit. The first lesson in this passage is to be obedient to the Holy Spirit.

Then we see that the devil waited until Jesus was physically weak to make any attacks. It wasn't until Jesus was in the desert for 40 days fasting that the devil came and tried to tempt him. Jesus could have chosen to fill himself physically, but He chose to feed His spirit first, rather than His flesh. Even in a time of extreme physical weakness, Jesus displayed great strength. This is amazing to me; I find myself getting irritable after one day of fasting, and often after just missing a single meal!

We also see that Satan's first attempt to tempt Jesus is to doubt His son-ship, and says, "*If* you are the son of God…" Satan still works this way today: if he can't prevent you from being saved, the first thing he will do is make you question your adoption by God, which would automatically put you under his kingdom of darkness. There are only two kingdoms, and all people are either under one or the other. If you do not believe you are saved through faith, the door is open for the devil. This temptation also shows how the devil tries to get Jesus to prove He is the son of God by performing a miracle. If Jesus had agreed, this would have been outside of God's will, and the Holy Spirit would not have honored the command. We cannot expect to perform miracles that are done only to prove to someone that God loves us. We have to know by faith, and we will perform miracles as the Holy Spirit leads us. God doesn't take orders from us; we take orders from Him. We do have authority over demons, but if you are testing God's love by demanding a miracle, you do not believe that you are saved through faith.

Satan's second attack on Jesus started the same way, "IF you are the son of God..." Satan already knew who Jesus was, but we notice how Satan was testing to see if Jesus REALLY knew who He was. Do you know who you are? Do you have a solid identity as a son/daughter of God? If you have confessed your sin before God, repented and turned from your sin, have been baptized (immersed) in water, and have been filled with the Holy Spirit, YOU ARE HIS. Even if you make a mistake after being saved, as long as you confess and repent, you are still right with God. You know when you are right with God. If you don't know for sure that you are right with God, pray for God to show you areas where you need to repent. Having your heart right with God and maintaining a clear conscience is very important to being ready for an attack from the enemy. This is the first area in which he will target. If he is able to dethrone you, it gives him a foot in the door.

The devil didn't give up after the first try; he tried three times to tempt Jesus before he finally left.

Let's note how Jesus says, "Away from me Satan! For it is written..." Jesus *commands* him to leave. He isn't praying and begging God to save Him from the devil. Jesus takes authority and tells Satan to go, following up with the true meaning of the Scripture. Without understanding, Scripture can be used to manipulate and deceive. Satan has been very successful in making many Christians look bad by making them believe false interpretations of the Scriptures. Satan will likewise test us to see if we have a mature understanding of God's word and its true meaning and application. Jesus corrected Satan and rebuked him with confidence and authority, as we should also do. Having the Holy Spirit is the only way to truly understand Scripture.

Notice how throughout this passage, the enemy is called the "devil", the "tempter", and "Satan". All three terms are interchangeable for the same entity.

We see that the devil twisted the meaning of the word of God twice and tried to get Jesus to doubt God, and finally, the devil resorted to promising Jesus power over the great kingdoms of the world, if only He would bow down and worship him instead of God. Satan owns all the kingdoms of this world, but Jesus has a better kingdom in heaven. Jesus uses His knowledge of the true meaning of God's word to overcome the devil. The devil's #1 objective is to be worshipped. Whether you do it unknowingly or do it willingly, he doesn't care. If you don't worship God, then the devil's got you. The devil is very powerful and cunning, and he does have the supernatural power to give you authority, but there is always a hidden price to pay, and it will always turn out to be a terrible curse, rather than a true blessing which comes only from God. God will always test and try you before making you a powerful leader so that you will have joy and be successful. There are no shortcuts to fame and fortune without deception.

If you don't worship God, then the devil's got you.

Jesus did not live by His feelings. He didn't do what he *felt* like doing whenever He felt like doing it. He considered the facts of what the devil was saying, He had faith in God's true meaning of His word, and His feelings followed. We cannot make decisions based on feelings, but need to live our lives based on

God's facts and choose to put the faith behind it so we can see God's truths manifest. Living by the truth of God's word and holding every thought "captive" to Christ will allow us to overcome the devil and live in the presence of God and under the blessing of God's promises. We cannot depend on what we see and experience in the natural world. Learning to live by faith in God's word takes time, study, and patience. The growth of our faith is fueled by trials, so stand firm in your faith; the rewards are life in the fullness of God, now and for eternity!

"Blessed is the one who perseveres under trial because, having stood the test, that person will receive the crown of life that the Lord has promised to those who love him."
James 1:12

Submit to God, Resist the Devil – We can overcome the power of the devil only when we first decide to submit ourselves before God, coming under His grace and will, and agree to His reign over our lives. When we come under God's kingdom, and pledge allegiance to Him and Him alone, we also inherit the blessings and protection of His kingdom. Without God's power and might, we are no match for Satan and his legions of demons. It is only possible to have victory over an invisible enemy with the help of invisible soldiers. God's angels will not be dispatched to those that have not come under God's authority. If you are trying to fight the devil on your own strength you will get tired very quickly! All the power you need to overcome is found in Jesus Christ through the working of the Holy Spirit. Look to the one who has overcome, and there you will find peace, and the ability to resist the devil.

"I have told you these things, so that in me you may have peace. In this world you will have trouble. But take heart! I have overcome the world." John 16:33

The second part of this verse tells us to resist the devil. To resist him, we need to first identify when it is the devil at work. Then we can reject the lie and embrace the truth of God's will over the situation. Whether we are being tempted by desire, or threatened with sickness or poverty, we can reject these outcomes and pray in the Holy Spirit for God's will.

Quoting Scripture over situations to show the devil we know what God's will is for us is helpful since most people sell God short and assume their problems are given by God for some higher purpose. Now this may be the case in certain situations, but the devil loves for us to blame God for our suffering so that we can stay there and never learn to live

Without the Holy Spirit, it will be difficult, if not impossible, to distinguish God's will over the lies of the enemy.

abundantly and totally trust God. God, of course, disciplines His children because He loves us, but let's not always assume that and let the devil off the hook so easily. What we should do, in all situations, is live by every word that comes from God, whether it is from reading the Bible or from personal revelation. God's ultimate desire is for us to obey His voice. The Bible tells us that faith comes by hearing, and hearing the word of God. This means you focus your time, not just reading the Bible, but hearing current stories about what amazing things God has done for people (their testimonies). It also means that you have a personal relationship with Him where you hear from Him directly, through prayer and worship. It means you are looking for answers from Him. Whether you have YouTube sermons playing, or an audio Bible reading to you, you are sure to pick up on lessons God wants to teach you.

The Holy Spirit will teach you how to apply God's Word to your life. Without the Holy Spirit, it will be difficult, if not impossible, to distinguish God's will over the lies of the enemy. The enemy wants you to do things too, so it is essential that you "submit yourselves" to your Bible and God's Truth so you can verify what you are hearing. Studying the Bible, and living by the Holy Spirit has an amazing result: it means you get to hear God's voice for yourself. No one can ever convince you that God is not real when this happens because it is so personal, but yet it is intangible. It's hard for non-believers to understand unless they've been anointed with the Holy Spirit as well. So when you are experiencing trials, remember the fourth chapter of James:

"Submit yourselves, then, to God. Resist the devil, and he will flee from you." James 4:7

Maintain Fellowship with God – This is the most important part of the gospel once you have been saved. The purpose of being forgiven by God is so that we may have a personal relationship with Him. He offers us His grace so that we might be drawn near to Him, despite our shortcomings and previous sins. All of us have sinned, and yet God created us in His image so that He might manifest His glory on earth. In order to maintain fellowship, or *right-standing* with God, we need to walk in the light. God never forces us to walk in the light, but we cannot claim to be Christians (Christ-Like-Ones), and still dabble from time to time in the dark. God will not work through us while we are double-minded.

"This is the message we have heard from him and declare to you: God is light; in him there is no darkness at all. If we claim to have fellowship with him and yet walk in the darkness, we lie and do not live out the truth. But if we walk in the light, as he is in the light, we have fellowship with one another, and the blood of Jesus, his Son, purifies us from all sin." 1 John 1:5-7

These are a few guidelines we can follow to make sure we stay in fellowship with God. This is the place from where all blessings flow, and in that place we can find peace, healing, comfort, and security. It is our choice to choose fellowship with Him over the fleeting pleasures of this world. It is our choice to put God first and commit ourselves to holy living. If we love our sin more than we love God, then it will show and we will be lukewarm and never walk under God's divine abundance, authority, and health.

Don't Be a Stranger – If you don't spend time with someone, they become distant and your relationship lacks intimacy. God's desire is to have a very personal relationship, and to be invited into each area of your life. He doesn't just want your prayer at the end of your day with lists of things you need and things for which you thank Him, He wants to be the central point in your life. He wants to be in all the details. And why wouldn't we want to glorify Him in all that we do? If God seems like a stranger to you, then it's probably because you don't spend time with Him. He tells us throughout the Old and New Testaments that He wants us to "obey His voice", and then He will be our God, and we will be His people. Obeying His voice is so much more than just reading the Bible, although you can obey His voice from reading the Bible, too. But God desires to speak to each one of us, and He seeks to guide us as a shepherd guides His flock – with His voice. Jesus says:

"My sheep listen to my voice; I know them, and they follow me." John 10:27

Do you listen to the voice of Jesus?
Do you think He knows you?
Do you obey Him and follow?
Or are you still in rebellion?

Being in rebellion means missing out on every wonderful thing God has planned for us. Let's not be deceived in thinking there is *anything* more precious than having an intimate relationship with God, or put a single thing in our lives in a higher position than Him. It is a lie from the enemy to think we can do otherwise and still be happy. We might be okay for a while, but eventually, things will catch up to us!

God desires to have a personal, two-way relationship with us, not that we give Him orders and He gives us orders, but a relationship like a father with his children, or a husband with his wife. It is very personal, loving, and compassionate, sharing the intimate beatings of your heart and all your hurts and pains. God wants to help us, heal us, and guide us into a life that is something we could have never attained without Him. He wants to know us and make us His people. He wants us to be kingdom-minded and be filled with His perfect peace and joy.

How would it glorify God for His people to suffer and be in poverty? It absolutely glorifies God when His people know Him, live in blessings and safety, and help others out of an overflow of His love. Spend time with God, quiet yourself, and hear what He has to say.

When I first got saved, and before I had developed my ability to hear God speak, I would pray for God to speak to me through His word, and then flip open the Bible randomly. I would always find exactly what I needed when I did this! Find something that works for you.

Be Obedient to God – Once you begin to hear God's voice, you have a choice: you can either obey what God tells you, or you can continue doing what you've always done which is going your own way. The definition of "wicked" in the Bible actually means, "going your own way". It doesn't necessarily mean that you are an evil person with bad intentions to harm others. Being "wicked" in God's eyes is doing anything that goes against what He would "will" (or desire) for you. It means you aren't on the narrow path, but rather on the wide path of many believers who think they are going the right direction, but are not really obeying God.

Dedicated Christians who seek, listen, and obey the voice of God are the biggest threat to the enemy. Take the time to ask God's view on ALL areas of your life, and then take the step and be obedient to Him. His direction will always line up with Scripture, so if you aren't sure it's God's voice, make sure it's always based in truth, presented in love, and that it is always for good.

Be Thankful in All Circumstances – No matter what is going on in your life, you always have access to the very throne room of the King of Kings, not even a prison cell can keep you from His divine presence. Joy comes from the Lord, and when things get too hard to stand, go ahead and kneel down. Your freedom and peace will come when you let your burden rest on His mighty shoulders.

Raising your thoughts into the heavenly realm and looking at your problems from those heights will give you a whole new perspective.

You can always find ways to thank God. Ascending into the heavens when times are hard takes self-discipline and faith, but it comes with amazing rewards. Raising your thoughts into the heavenly realm and looking at your problems from those heights will give you a whole new perspective. You'll also have the opportunity to seek God's counsel, and He will lead you with His Holy Spirit, giving you strength and endurance. Persevere in those times, pressing into God and thinking about the things for which you actually ARE thankful. I'm not saying that if you lose a loved one, you thank God for that, but rather you might thank Him for your children, or your health, or your job.

Be honest with God. You don't need to hide your feelings; He already knows what is on your heart anyway.

You know when I sit and when I rise; you perceive my thoughts from afar. Psalm 139:2

Because Jesus lived and suffered, He is the perfect High Priest to discuss these matters and comfort you, as He can relate with you in all things. We know that even as Jesus suffered, He never allowed it to push Him into sin, so He is the perfect one to look to for an example of how to address your specific concern.

Being thankful to God for His previous acts of faithfulness to you also helps. I know that when miracles happen it is very exciting at first, but it wears off! It is a nice exercise to try and make it a point to remember these things when you are experiencing troubles, for it gives you hope that God will also see you through your current situation. Keeping your mind thankful and not allowing yourself to become negative and hopeless is a powerful tool in overcoming the enemy and his attacks. God IS big enough to handle whatever the enemy throws at you.

Spend Time in Prayer, Study, and Worship

Worship of God is one of the most powerful weapons you have against the enemy and his minions. Demons HATE it when you praise God – they just can't stand it! They have to flee! Keep in mind: demons want you to get mad at God. They want you to doubt Him and doubt yourself and work yourself up into a frenzy of anxiety and fear. But remaining positive and actually cranking up the radio and just praising God is the best medicine for you! I tell you; this is my favorite way to overcome the enemy. Seriously! It's fun, and it's really good exercise if you let yourself dance, put your arms up and REALLY get INTO it! Go ahead and cry and worship and pour your heart out to God! He loves you so much! Don't let the enemy make you think for a second that God has forgotten you! You just remind that devil whose son or daughter you are, and that you believe every word that comes out of God's mouth. Prayer is also another powerful tool, which is of course your offensive weapon against the enemy. Jesus tells us:

"I will give you the keys of the kingdom of heaven; whatever you bind on earth will be bound in heaven, and whatever you loose on earth will be loosed in heaven." Matthew 16:19

If you aren't sure how to proceed but you know there is demonic activity around you, you can bind up those impure spirits until you get confirmation through the Holy Spirit on how to move forward. There's no point in Jesus giving us authority if we never use it. When we dedicate ourselves to the hearing of God's Word, studying the Bible, worshipping God, and

You cannot expect to see miracles and enter into the Promised Land when you are not spending time with God.

practicing His principles in our lives, we will become stronger and stronger with time.

With dedication, your faith will grow and grow, and so will your confidence. Without dedication, you are really opening yourself up for trouble. You cannot expect to see miracles and enter into the Promised Land when you are not spending time with God. He knows when your heart is in it and when it's not. Sometimes it takes months, and hours and hours of prayer and worship to see results. Don't give up. God listens to every prayer, and just as Daniel had to wait 3 weeks for the answer to his prayer, even with much prayer and fasting, the angel that God sent with the answer to Daniel's prayer had to go through demonic attacks before it arrived to deliver the answer. God ALWAYS answers our prayers. Now that we have the Holy Spirit, our prayers are even more efficiently delivered! Do not doubt God, but rather, keep pressing in and seeking God's will over everything in your life, in your country, and in the world. Speak God's will over your life and it will begin to manifest into reality.

Fellowship with the Body of Christ

The *church* is fellow believers that make up the Body of Christ. We are called to gather and worship God together, bear each other's burdens, study together, and to become disciples. Being part of a group of fellow believers can be intimidating at first. Chances are, everyone else is feeling the same way you are, and all have their own struggles of one kind or another. There will always be that ebb and flow, of some people being on the mountaintop sometimes, and other times down in the valley. Let us be gracious people and fulfill God's commandment of loving our

If you are offended by someone, you haven't died to yourself.

neighbor as ourselves. We need to be there to celebrate with others when they are at the top, and to also be there to listen and encourage our fellow believers when they are down low.

The thing I look for most in a church (besides, of course, sound doctrine and belief in the spiritual gifts), is whether or not I like the music. I may not like every song, but I want to really worship God in a way that I feel comfortable. Many churches these days offer a traditional service in the morning and a more upbeat, contemporary service mid-morning and even in the evenings.

Going to church is probably not where you will connect with people. Get involved with a ministry, Sunday School class, Bible Study group, or other volunteer position so that you can make friends and fellowship with other believers. I personally like to have friends of all ages; the younger ones to encourage, the ones my age to relate and study with, and the ones who are a little older and more mature in their faith from whom I can learn and seek guidance when necessary.

Resolving conflicts is a skill that is Biblical and shows that you are a mature Christian. Whenever you are around other people - Christians are no exception - there will be conflict. But we aren't allowed to be offended. If you are offended by someone, you haven't died to yourself. We should be crying for that person, not because of them. If they knew how much God loves them, they probably would not have acted the way they did. Think about it. People act wrongly because they are insecure; and usually it's because they don't know their identity in Christ and are still trying to prove something to someone, or be right, or not be wrong, or whatever. The truth is, even if someone is wrong and even extremely unlikable, they are still God's child just like you. You aren't better than anyone else. Jesus died for your sins as well as theirs. It is only by grace that we are saved, not because of anyone's works or deeds, so none of us have the right to boast!

We are called to love the unlovable, just as God loves them (and us); not by accepting their sin, but by agreeing with God that nothing is stopping us from loving them and being kind to them.

Now, of course, there are exceptions to this if someone is abusing you or breaking the law, but most of the time, conflicts within a church body are because people don't know their identity in Christ. It's true some people are easy to love, but with time, all their imperfections come out. You can either judge them, or do what James tells us: don't stand on the law and be a judge, and thereby bring judgment on yourself! Don't let fear keep you from church. Getting involved with a church group gives you a place to worship, volunteer, learn, and grow.

Agree with God

If we want our Elohim (God our Creator) to dwell within us, we need to dwell with Him. It is hard to dwell with anyone when you are in disagreement. If you have ever raised a teenager you know it is hard to live with a child who is in rebellion against you! We need to cultivate self-discipline in agreeing with God. So, although the word "discipline" may scare you a bit, it's really beneficial for you to understand and admit the fact that you are part of a world where discipline is a necessary thing that actually provides safety, security, and peace. If we are disciplined and know that God wants to heal people and set them free from demonic torment then we are better able to combat the enemy.

Our goal is to be in agreement with God about His will for us and for others. We MUST know that God desires for us all to be His. It saddens God that some people ARE perishing. He gave us free will, out of love, so that we are not robots programmed to love, but, instead, choose to love Him and walk in His ways. God wants to bless us if we would only come and repent.

The Lord is not slow in keeping his promise, as some understand slowness. Instead he is patient with you, not wanting anyone to perish, but everyone to come to repentance. 2 Peter 3:9

God wants us to love Him and love each other. He wants us to reach out to the lost and forgotten people of the world and show them His crazy, ridiculous, supernatural love. Each one of us is created in the image of God, but each of us has the free will to choose good or evil. We can choose whether we want to live to restore the world, or to cause destruction. In Matthew 16, Jesus tells people about the Kingdom of Heaven, and He explains that if we do something to help someone, it is like doing it for God Himself. AND that if we see someone in need and do not help him, it is like NOT helping God Himself.

Let's not be lazy, but instead, realize that we are expected to be a light, and that everywhere we go and everything we do is being watched and evaluated, if we are claiming to be Christians. We might be the only "Jesus" someone ever meets. It may be just a small seed of love that we plant in someone's broken heart that grows into a mighty ministry.

We might be the only "Jesus" someone ever meets.

Compassion and love grow when we are accountable to God for all our actions, come under the discipline of God and His commandments, and begin to truly understand the love God has for us. When we are filled with the love and Spirit of God, we can then overflow to others. If we aren't filled with God's love and Spirit, then all our "works" are more for ourselves than for others and/or God. God gives us everything we need to do all good works, and will provide anything He wants us to bestow upon others, according to His perfect will.

"But seek first his kingdom and his righteousness, and all these things will be given to you as well." Matthew 6:33

If we can put God's Kingdom first and live free in His Righteousness, then we will walk in God's love and not focus on money, food, physical appearance, clothes, or whatever else we obsess about that really has no value to us. God knows we need all these things, and if we stop doubting Him, and get our heart where it needs to be, He will be able to help!

As long as we are still living for us and trying to benefit ourselves, we aren't really filled with God's love, and He knows. We can't trick Him. We really need to surrender to Him one hundred percent, die to ourselves, and come under His authority. Without this piece, you really don't have authority over demons, for it is only "He that is in you is stronger than he who is in the world." If you don't know for sure that, "He is in you" (the Holy Spirit of God), and He isn't KING of your life, then something else is "king" in your life that rules over you. Being under *authority* of God won't make temptations completely go away, but they will never rule over you again.

Walking in Spirit and Truth means that we are in *daily* obedience to the leading of the Holy Spirit, and that we spend time *daily* in the study of His Word. We are welcomed into the Kingdom of Light and sealed with His Holy Spirit once we believe, but being led by the Holy Spirit is something we need to ask for each day. It is a constant battle between our will and God's will. Paul explains it like this:

Those who live according to the flesh have their minds set on what the flesh desires; but those who live in accordance with the Spirit have their minds set on what the Spirit desires.

The mind governed by the flesh is death, but the mind governed by the Spirit is life and peace. Romans 8:5-6

Victory is won when we: submit to God and His leading and resist every other force that comes against us. These opposing forces could be the culture of the world, our fleshly and selfish desires, or from the demonic realm. It is up to us to develop awareness to what is going on in our own lives and choose to stand firming on the Word of God.

CHAPTER 7

Come Under Discipline

When you are born again, you become born of the Spirit of God. You are a new creation in Christ who saved you. This new spiritual being needs spiritual food to live, and that food is God's Word. Jesus says He is the bread of life, and we must eat His teachings up if we want to grow and mature in our faith. One of the things that happen when we are saved is that we agree with God about our sin. We know God loves us, but He doesn't like our sin, and neither should we. We should apply Godly principals to all areas of our lives.

To God – This includes God's leading through the Holy Spirit, devoting yourself to prayer, respecting and maintaining love to others, and following the Ten Commandments – the First Commandment being to put God first and love nothing more than God. Want to know how much you love God? How much do you love His Word (the Bible)? However much you love His Word and Truth is a good indicator of how much you love God! If you love His Word, you will spend time ready, studying, and pondering it. You cannot be really "in love" with someone if you don't constantly want to be with them – it is the same with your relationship with God.

However much you love His Word and Truth is a good indicator of how much you love God!

If you are thirsty for His Word and starving to death until you can eat up His spiritual food, then you should be in a good place. If the Bible is dull and dry, you probably haven't spent much time in it, or you haven't spent much time in passionate worship and prayer to have it touch your heart.

There's no way you can really meet Jesus and not be totally transformed and in love. We come under His authority not because of fear, but because of the awesomeness of His love. We are filled with love and peace just being in His presence. Having a direct connection with the King of Kings and Creator of the universe is not something you can compare with a new pair of shoes, a new car, or even a new house. It is beyond *awesome* to be in His presence, and you will not want to do anything to screw up that relationship. Plenty of people say they love God, but they don't show it by spending time to study His word.

To Yourself (Self-Discipline) – Letting the Holy Spirit lead you rather than being led by your flesh is another marker of conversion into Christ. This can be assessed by the way you conduct yourself, your speech, the way you take care of yourself, and where you spend your time. What are your priorities? Do you think it's important to spend time in study, worship, and prayer? Do you share your faith, or keep it to yourself? Do you love the body God gave you and take care of it with healthy food, exercise, and abstaining from unhealthy substances like drugs, alcohol, and excess sugar? Do you honor God with your finances? Don't forget the parable about the manager who entrusted money to His servants and came back expecting the money to have grown. God gives us money and expects us to do well with it, not wasting it, but, instead, sowing it wisely and making it grow. The baptism of the Holy Spirit will lead you in a character change that will effect every area of your life, and we need to be obedient to follow. Just practicing self-control doesn't make you a Christian, but the in-dwelling Holy Spirit will help you become self-disciplined.

To Your Government – This is referring to following the laws of the land. Although all the kingdoms of this world are controlled by Satan (as we read about in Matthew, Chapter 4), God expects us to be upright citizens. It doesn't mean that the laws of the land determine moral standards (God is the only one who can do that.), but you need to follow the rules, such as traffic laws, not stealing or shoplifting, paying taxes, respecting other people's rights, etc. We need to pray for our leaders to make decisions that align with God's Word, after binding the impure spirits that control them. We still need to

Remember, our battles are not against persons with bodies, but rather the spirits that influence the leaders.

respect the laws of the land even if we don't agree with them. There are spiritual and legal ways to bring change and stand up for what is right in God's eyes. Remember, our battles are not against persons with bodies, but rather the spirits that influence the leaders. If we can deliver the people, then we will save souls and help people be free from the grip of the enemy. We should be as Christians going against corrupt governments, and protecting those that can't protect themselves. There are Godly ways of change and man's way of bringing change, and we should follow God's leading, always seeking confirmation of His direction. Jesus knows that, one day, He will reign over all the kingdoms of the earth, and we need to start preparing the ways for that to happen by collectively praying and binding the "principal and authority spirits" in the Name of Jesus and casting them out.

To Your Marriage – Marriage is a gift that God designed. It is a blessed union between a man and a woman who are equally paired, each having specific roles to fulfill. In God's eyes they are considered one. A man is designed as the provider and protector, and the woman as the nurturer and helper. Of course there is much more to it, but the point I want to make here is that the man is head of the marriage, just like God is the head of Christ. (1 Corinthians 11:3) Neither one is better than the other or more important yet both serve specific functions. The Holy Spirit is also called the "helper", and serves to fulfill God's will and strengthen His people. Women should stop being prideful and assuming that the helper is something degraded or insignificant. The man needs a helper! God saw that it wasn't good for man to be alone, so He created the woman. We need each other, and we need to embrace our role and stop fighting against it.

The Lord God said, "It is not good for the man to be alone. I will make a helper suitable for him." Genesis 2:18

Whenever the marriage relationship is out of whack, we are not acting in the will of God (for example, a man not stepping up and leading, or a woman trying to lead or dominate her husband). There are times when a husband needs his wife to lead, like when he is overly stressed or ill, but generally women are expected to let the man be the head. Men also can grant leadership to women in certain areas, so it's not like women can't have any responsibility. It is when one person takes on the responsibility or role of the other that causes a problem. It is a tendency, especially in America, for a woman to dominate her husband and treat him like he is another one of her children. It's no wonder so many marriages end in divorce.

Men desire respect, and women desire love. Of course both parties need both love and respect, and this topic could become a book in itself. For more on this topic for women, I highly recommend, Created to Be His Help Meet by Debi Pearl. For men, the book Created to Need a Help Meet by Michael Pearl is excellent.

121

You are opening yourself up for trouble with the enemy if you are a woman dominating your husband or if you are a man who is not leading your family in a Godly way. No one should "dominate" the other. We should, instead, accept our roles as God designed them, and seek for His headship in all areas of our life, especially in marriage. If you have a problem with "headship", you may be in rebellion against God as well. If you are His child and love Him, you will also love what God loves: a Godly view on marriage.

As hard as this one is to accept for many people (as it was for me in the beginning), it comes with so many blessings. For me personally, letting God direct my marriage was what saved my marriage. After I was converted, my old ways just didn't set right with me. All of a sudden, it wasn't about what was wrong, it was about what God could do through me to make positive changes. It wasn't about everything the other person wasn't doing, it was about me getting myself together and bringing everything I had to the table, being under God's authority whether I liked it or not.

The first thing God asked me to do to show my faith was to iron my husband's clothes (Which I did once, and, thankfully, God never asked me to do again!). I wrestled with this direction from God and at first just rejected it. "No way!" I thought.

Eventually, after a day of arguing with God, I went ahead and did it. My husband came home from work and was not sure what to think. He thought I had lost my mind or just wanted something! I had to explain to my husband that I am here to serve, not to be served.

The message sent through this act of obedience to God was this, "I love you, and I'm here to help you. I'm here to serve, not to be served. Please take care of me and protect me. I need you to lead." I'm not sure how that all was silently communicated with me ironing his clothes ONCE, but nevertheless, God was in all of it and it really was a turning point for us. Now I do all kinds of things for my husband, not simply because God tells me to, but because I love my husband and want to glorify God in all that I do. I know God wants me to be kind and give grace, lifting up my husband and helping Him wherever I possibly can. My husband didn't lead in many areas before this because I didn't let him! Ladies, you have to get out of the way and let your husbands lead! It's not right for you to lead your home or talk badly about or to your husband. Marriage is just like the relationship between Jesus and the church - a husband should love and care for his wife just like Jesus loves and cherishes His bride, the church, and a wife should love and serve her husband just as the church is supposed to serve the Lord.

Marriage is a sacred covenant before God, and if you are a Christian but do not follow God's blueprint for marriage, you are asking for heartache, frustration, and trouble. It feels really good to be able to be a woman and not constantly try and prove myself by trying to act like a man. I need my man to be a man, and my man needs me to be a woman.

To Your Family – It will go well with you to respect the elders in your family. "Honor your Mother and Father," doesn't add, "but only if they deserve it"! It just says, "Honor your Mother and Father so that it may go well with you and you will enjoy a long life." It is the only commandment that comes along with a blessing. It also hints at a curse that if you do not honor them, that you are not going to live a long life. No matter what kind of parents you have, you can still choose whether or not to speak kindly of them. (Remember we don't wrestle against flesh and blood.) Can you imagine your own children speaking badly about you? It's just not right whatever your circumstance may be.

You've got to honor your parents by showing them respect and treating them kindly. You may be in a situation where it is unsafe to be around your parents, and that is fine, you need to stay safe, but what I am talking about is speaking badly and holding anger in your heart. The enemy will use this against you with such force, and you will always question God's love for you. Luckily, our Father in Heaven is a good Father, but our relationship with Him cannot necessarily be deepening if we see Him the same way we see our earthly fathers. What we can do is seek a relationship with God and try to see our parents through God's eyes, casting our burdens at His feet, constantly reminding ourselves that God loves us perfectly. It is hard to love others and walk rightly if you don't feel loved by God. And any kind of rejection you may have felt from your parents will likely affect your relationship with God.

What I am encouraging you to do, is to bring your relationship with your parents (and/or in-laws), under God's authority. Always acting and speaking in love, and biting your tongue, or keeping your distance until you are mature enough to handle your parental situation. The only opinion you need to worry about is God's opinion. If you try to please everyone, you'll never get anywhere. If you let God lead you, it will all be okay! It takes time to restore relationships and for people to realize you aren't the same you. You're a new creation in Christ!

The only opinion you need to worry about is God's opinion.

You may feel like you need to prove yourself, but this isn't true either. We don't have much good to offer anyone on our own; but with Christ in us- the hope of glory- we can overflow with the love of Jesus and earn the love and admiration of people that once hated us. You don't need to worry about pleasing people, but instead choose to please God. By wanting to please God, it makes it a whole lot easier to love people that are mean to you. God is worth pleasing. In fact, He loves you so much that He gave His Son in order to purchase you from the hands of the devil! God says you are worth it! If God didn't think you were worth it, why did Heaven pay such a high price for you? You need not strive to prove yourself, but rather to realize that you don't need to; no one can earn God's favor except through faith in Jesus. Then we can receive His Spirit and begin to walk rightly. You can improve through God's help and strength through the Holy Spirit, and without Him, you can do nothing.

Put to death, therefore, whatever belongs to your earthly nature: sexual immorality, impurity, lust, evil desires and greed, which is idolatry. Because of these, the wrath of God is coming. You used to walk in these ways, in the life you once lived. But now you must also rid yourselves of all such things as these: anger, rage, malice, slander, and filthy language from your lips. Do not lie to each other, since you have taken off your old self with its practices and have put on the new self, which is being renewed in knowledge in the image of its Creator. Colossians 3:5-10

We are called to love and forgiveness, and a seared conscience cannot walk in love. Being under God's authority can also refer to us as parents. Are we acting as Godly parents to our children? Are we teaching God's precepts to them and praising God? Are we being kind and generous to others, stopping to help a neighbor or friend, volunteering our time, and praying for the sick?

A little love goes a long way, and letting our children see us act in Godly ways will have more of an impact on them than taking them to Sunday school. I think Sunday school and classes are great, but for them to make an impact, we must make it a part of our life, our way of life. Lifestyle Christians love God and love people, no matter how they may be treated in return. It is a fine line between lovingly guiding our children and

To be holy is to be dedicated to God.

125

disciplining them too harshly, but God has given us His Holy Spirit to guide us and lead us. We have access to every resource we need through the Holy Spirit. When we dedicate ourselves to God, God will be faithful to His word. To be *holy* is to be *dedicated* to God. Let us turn to Him in all our needs and look to Him for the answers. The world has much to tell us about how we are to think and live, but God, alone, knows what is really best for us, and what will make us truly happy.

To Godly Thoughts – Your thoughts are where the enemy will attack first. You've got to offer up your whole body to God as a living sacrifice (including your mind), grabbing each thought and holding it accountable to God's Truth. You must reject each ungodly thought, and grab the promises of God instead.

"Therefore, I urge you, brothers and sisters, in view of God's mercy, to offer your bodies as a living sacrifice, holy and pleasing to God—this is your true and proper worship. Do not conform to the pattern of this world, but be transformed by the renewing of your mind. Then you will be able to test and approve what God's will is—his good, pleasing and perfect will." Romans 12:1-2

The enemy whispers in our ear and bombards us with lies. We must choose to turn to God, and listen to His voice instead. God doesn't dominate us or shove things down our throats. God loves us and wants us to obey out of love and respect for Him. But we need to make an effort, and realize that spiritual warfare starts in

The enemy whispers in our ear and bombards us with lies. We must choose to turn to God, and listen to His voice instead.

our minds, and it starts with Satan trying to make us doubt God, or even blame God for the bad things that happen to us. Yes, God disciplines us sometimes, but not every hard thing we endure is God's discipline. The enemy comes to steal, kill, and destroy.

If we are not watchful and prepared for the enemy's attacks, we are probably falling asleep. We've got to know God's word and apply it to our lives. It does nothing just sitting on the pages of a book. We've got to pray and use God's Word! The blood of the lamb at the first Passover did nothing to protect the people until it was applied to the lintel (or door posts) of the home. And it wouldn't have done any good, either, if the people hadn't stayed inside the house. Don't go outside of God's house and expect nothing bad to happen. We triumph over the enemy by applying the blood to our lives and by the word of our testimony that we have died and been risen again in the newness of life by the Holy Spirit. Visiting our past apart from the blood of Jesus is to invite a spirit of offense into our present reality. We must live in the present moment knowing that we are alive in Christ.

They triumphed over him by the blood of the Lamb and by the word of their testimony; they did not love their lives so much as to shrink from death. Revelation 12:11

Finding Joy

There is such joy and peace found in having a right relationship with our Creator. Shame, guilt, and fear have no place in our lives when we come into the presence of our ABBA Father God.

People rebel because they think they will find happiness in something other than God, and whatever that thing is becomes an idol. The enemy would love for you to believe that you won't have happiness or joy if you devote yourself to God. Brothers and sisters, joy comes from the Lord! You cannot be in God's presence and rule with Him in heavenly places and not have joy!

God's people are supposed to look different from the world. This book wasn't written to scare anyone into thinking demons are lurking around every corner. It doesn't mean they aren't, but really, wherever the Lord is, the demons aren't. What kind of impression does it give to non-believers if you call yourself a Christian and walk around like a nervous wreck? That isn't going to make anyone excited to hear about Jesus. Christianity should be attractive! God is awesome! His praise should always be on our lips!

The joy of the Lord is your strength. With everything that the enemy is trying to do to the people of God there is always something to grieve about. Times are hard and they aren't going to get better until the Lord returns. However, we can have joy amongst the tribulation if our joy is found in Him. Whether you are swept off to heaven or just praising God in your secret place, you can have joy. Joy is what attracted me to want to know the Lord in the first place. Before I was saved I attended a Bible Study and the women there had joy. I figured they just were blessed and had no problems in their life. The truth was, they had problems just like everybody else, but their joy and peace was based on their relationship with God rather than based on their circumstances. Their house was built on the rock, so when the waves came, they just stood firm and let the waves swell and pound. They were firmly grounded in the joy of the Lord, and I wanted it, too.

When you focus on God instead of on your problems, the atmosphere will change.

You'll need that joy to bring you through troubles. When you focus on God instead of on your problems, the atmosphere will change. Don't let the enemy steal your joy. Focus on your blessings, Jesus, and God's Word and promises. When you get caught up in emotional chaos and let yourself get so stressed out you can't function, that is the time to drop everything and get down on the floor and pray. We are commanded not to worry!

"Therefore I tell you, do not worry about your life, what you will eat or drink; or about your body, what you will wear. Is not life more than food, and the body more than clothes? Look at the birds of the air; they do not sow or reap or store away in barns, and yet your heavenly Father feeds them. Are you not much more valuable than they? Can any one of you by worrying add a single hour to your life? Matthew 6:25-27

When you are discouraged, read psalms and how much God loves you. Read the books written to the Corinthians. Read Philippians 4:4-9, my personal favorite, which always brings me back to the truth and peace of God. Worship God and play uplifting Christian music. Find something to thank God for, and try to live from a place that is in heaven with your Father God right there holding your hand. You aren't alone, and He won't let you go. Only God can give you rest, but you've got to come to Him. If you lay all that stuff down at His feet and trust Him to guide you through it, He will give you back something, and that something is JOY. So open up that gift right now!

What you have in this life will carry on into eternity so grab onto joy and don't let it go! When you look to God to help you through and become Kingdom-minded, you can't help but be happy. The peace and joy of God is just weird, and it doesn't make any sense. You can be walking through a situation that is like walking through a tunnel of fire where everyone is freaking out, but you are barely even warm from the blazing flames and are certainly not getting burned. With God, just like Shadrach, Meshach and Abednego, we can be thrown into the flames and not be burned. Our God will save us, and on top of that, we will have His joy!

Being in the Lord's presence is to overcome the enemy. The enemy can't be in God's presence! No demon of cancer, allergies, asthma, Ebola, addiction, gluttony, depression, anxiety, or anything else can live in the Lord's presence. If you raise your thoughts, and spend time in the throne room with God and live from that place of looking at life from heaven's perspective, your life will be transformed. The time is now! Start putting God first in your life. He is looking for people that want to be used to bring in the harvest. But it's not about wanting to be with Him so He'll give you what you want. You've got to delight yourself in the Lord, and don't worry about anything else. It is a lie of the enemy that anything God could GIVE you is better than being WITH God. Just being with Him is the greatest gift you could ever receive.

If you love God with ALL your heart and put Him first, His love will fill you, and you'll be able to love the people in your life even more. It is a lie from the enemy to think you have to tell your children, wife, or your husband that you love them the most. At first this sounds crazy, but if you explain it to them they will start to get it. And maybe, just maybe, they will imitate you! Wouldn't it be a blessing if your children and spouse loved God more than anything? God wants us to find balance in our life (which is a whole other book in itself). It will bring you much joy to put God first. You'll also find that you become more productive and that life gets easier for you. It sure did for me. Make time for God. Don't wait until you have a few extra minutes – make time for

Don't worry about the "stuff" you think will make you happy, but focus, instead, on the One from Whom happiness actually comes.

Him. Make it your number ONE priority every day to spend time with God, and live for Him. If your spouse told you they loved you but never spent any time with you, would you feel loved? God is looking for a bride that attends to Him, and in return He attends to her. God's people will stand out and be more successful, healthier, and have more of everything (especially joy) because they have Him. Don't worry about the "stuff" you think will make you happy, but focus, instead, on the One from Whom happiness actually comes. All truly good gifts come from the Father.

When I say, "Joy comes from the Lord," I'm not saying we should be happy about bad things that happen. What I am saying is that we can find joy through knowing God. We can trust Him and know that everything is going to be okay, and that even when bad things happen He will teach us how to make it work for good.

Even if you don't *feel* okay, remember, you can't live by feelings – you need to live by faith. Knowing who you are in Christ will change your life. If you seek God in all things, your light will shine so brightly that it will attract others and point them to the Lord.

Don't ever let the enemy remind you of your past mistakes and feel guilty. Your joy comes from the Lord Jesus Christ. Joy comes in knowing that you are forgiven and free, and no longer under the curse of the law. You are God's beloved.

CHAPTER 8

Jesus's Ministry

Then Peter began to speak: "I now realize how true it is that God does not show favoritism but accepts from every nation the one who fears him and does what is right. You know the message God sent to the people of Israel, announcing the good news of peace through Jesus Christ, who is Lord of all. You know what has happened throughout the province of Judea, beginning in Galilee after the baptism that John preached—how God anointed Jesus of Nazareth with the Holy Spirit and power, and how he went around doing good and healing all who were under the power of the devil, because God was with him. Acts 10:34-38

Jesus's mission is to bring people from the kingdom of darkness into the Kingdom of Light. There were people who loved Him and others who were under the power of the devil that hated Him. Jesus was persecuted by His own people and the church for delivering and healing people. They crucified Him. I also experienced persecution from people in my home church when God began healing and delivering people through me. It's not that they reject us *personally*, but they deny the power of Jesus Christ that is working through us. Some people even claim the supernatural workings of God are from demons! Since when did the devil heal cancer or make a blind person see? Since when did the devil cast out a devil?

Jesus was driving out a demon that was mute. When the demon left, the man who had been mute spoke, and the crowd was amazed. But some of them said, "By Beelzebul, the prince of demons, he is driving out demons." Others tested him by asking for a sign from heaven. Luke 11:14-16

The main people that accused Jesus of being empowered by the enemy were the church leaders, but as we see in the above verse, some people in the crowd thought the same thing! Believers today have fallen so far away from what the True Gospel is all about. The result is that they do not have fellowship with God, and they have become lukewarm.

In most Bible accounts, deliverance and healing were recorded together. Demons are the cause of many sicknesses and disease. As children of God, Jesus gives us authority to drive these spirits out and command healing. The healing authority of God is available to all of us through the Holy Spirit. No one owns these gifts. It's not our power that does the work; it is the power of Christ in us: the Holy Spirit. After Jesus was resurrected, He went to visit the apostles, and the very last thing He told them before He ascended to Heaven was this:

He said to them, "Go into all the world and preach the gospel to all creation. Whoever believes and is baptized will be saved, but whoever does not believe will be condemned. And these signs will accompany those who believe: In my name they will drive out demons; they will speak in new tongues; they will pick up snakes with their hands; and when they drink deadly poison, it will not hurt them at all; they will place their hands on sick people, and they will get well." Mark 16:15-18

The last words that anyone makes before they die are usually profound and of extreme importance. Have you experienced any of these signs? Do you really believe? Have faith! If you haven't, don't worry, you will soon. Just keep pressing into God because He wants you to want to learn these things.

Jesus came and lived as a man more than just to give you salvation, more than just to give you the keys of heaven, more than just to give you authority over demons; He also came to show you how to live by faith. He came to show you how to live everyday: how to treat people, how to manage your finances, how to devote yourself to prayer, teaching, and worship. Jesus has a wonderful plan for you and wants to lead you as a good shepherd cares for His sheep. Jesus will lead you beside quiet waters and refresh your soul. He will heal your body and give you an inheritance if only you will obey His voice!

The following verse promises physical health to your WHOLE body to those who read God's word and focus on them. There are many promises of PHYSICAL healing in the Bible, but this one is my favorite because there is no way it could mean anything besides what it says – God's words bring health to one's whole body. Have faith brothers and sisters, your miracle is coming!

My son, pay attention to what I say; turn your ear to my words. Do not let them out of your sight, keep them within your heart; for they are life to those who find them and health to one's whole body. Proverbs 4:20-22

If you do not think that healing for you is possible, it probably isn't. If you believe that it is, it probably is. What you believe is what will happen to you. Do you think God is not willing to heal you? Or do you just assume because you haven't already been healed that it isn't God's will to heal you? Here is a case just like that in the Bible and Jesus WAS WILLING. You've come to the HEALER Himself. Of course He wants to heal you! Do you want to be healed? Jesus is the same yesterday, today and tomorrow. There isn't one case in the Bible where Jesus said "No" to healing or where He *couldn't* heal someone.

When Jesus came down from the mountainside, large crowds followed him. A man with leprosy came and knelt before him and said, "Lord, if you are willing, you can make me clean." Jesus reached out his hand and touched the man. "I am willing," he said. "Be clean!" Immediately he was cleansed of his leprosy. Matthew 8:1-3

We see from this verse that the man came to Him and knelt before Jesus. He came humbly asking for help. He was not supposed to be around other people, but you see the man joined a large crowd of people. Usually lepers were expected to stay away from people in case they were contagious. But the man was desperate. The enemy had afflicted this man - for how long we do not know - but as soon as He asked Jesus for help, even accepting that God's will could've been "No," Jesus healed him. Jesus immediately and completely healed the man's disease.

I watched something similar to this happen once on my son's skin when he was little (not leprosy, but a skin wound). He was playing, and his face got pinched by a Nerf gun. It was immediately purple, and there was a blood blister, too. He was screaming in pain. I held him and prayed to God, and I commanded his skin to be healed, just like Jesus did in the situation with the leper ("Be clean!" is what Jesus said, I just changed it to "Be healed!"). I also told his pain to stop. I did this very quietly because there were people around, and, at that point, I was still unsure about all of this God-healing stuff. He immediately stopped crying. About an hour later, I picked him up and was shocked to see that his face was clear! No bruising, no blood blister, it was completely healed! So if it works for me, it will work for you. If you have the Holy Spirit and a little bit of faith, you can do what Jesus did, just like I did. Jesus is alive and well, and if you focus on Him and His teachings, you can do everything He did and more. Jesus encourages us in this truth:

"Very truly I tell you, whoever believes in me will do the works I have been doing, and they will do even greater things than these, because I am going to the Father."
John 14:12

Jesus helps us in hopes that we will also help others. I have heard of stories where people have been healed, but lost their healing after a time. This is because they never praised God and testified to others about His goodness. God didn't just heal us so we can continue in a selfish lifestyle. I was healed of sciatic pain and also from back injuries caused by a car accident. At that point in my life, there was nothing doctors could do, no treatments left to perform, I was considered a chronic pain sufferer, and all they could do was help me manage my pain. It was horrible.

My entire life revolved around this identity. My moods would surge if my pain medication wore off, and if I took too much, I would throw up. Even with medication, I still had pain all the time, and eventually I became really depressed. Because of the injury and the pain I couldn't hike or ski anymore and I gained a bunch of weight so that even swimming was uncomfortable. I was just a wreck. Then all of a sudden, I realized that Jesus healed ALL who came to Him. So I figured, why not me? God certainly didn't cause me to be hit by a drunk driver. There was no lesson or refinement going on there. It was pure suffering. One day I was watching a show called "Sid Roth, It's Supernatural," and at first I thought it was kind of silly. But there was a man on the show sharing testimonies of people being healed from back problems. He finished up with a prayer for everyone watching, and at that moment, I was healed! It was instant! I also was able to get off the pain medication that same moment and with no mood swings, which is a miracle, too, because they were the addictive kind. After that, I praised God and have been healed and pain-free ever since. I had such a dramatic life change that I told God I wanted to help other people be healed, too.

I prayed for Him to use me as His vessel to help people. And He did! After that, there were a bunch of people who I just happened to connect with, and somehow we got on the topic of their back problems. God healed all of them! They weren't all instantly healed, and some of them I had to tell bad spirits to leave before they could be healed. But they all were healed within a short period of time. I didn't give up on praying for people if they weren't healed instantly, and you shouldn't either. With one individual, the pain went completely away, but the injury remained. It wasn't until two months later that I saw them and found out they *had* been delivered and gotten their healing. Then they asked me how they could become a Christian, and I explained the Gospel to them and they gave their life to Jesus right there in front of my eyes! After we prayed for the Holy Spirit to come upon him, he immediately felt the peace of God. It was a true miracle. You never know what seed a little prayer will plant.

I wanted to share my testimony because I knew that it would help people's faith, and God brought me people who were at a point where they wanted to know the Healer and be healed. I was healed after hearing people's testimonies of supernatural healing because then I had the faith to believe I could be healed. I figured that if I shared my story, it would produce the same faith in them, and they were healed! It worked! In the book of Matthew, Jesus tells His disciples that when they go out preaching the good news of the kingdom, that they should also share their testimony, that whatever they have received, they should give. His message still applies today! If you received deliverance, help others! If you have received physical healing, pray for others to be healed!

"Heal the sick, raise the dead, cleanse those who have leprosy, drive out demons. Freely you have received; freely give."
Matthew 10:8

The next story from Jesus's ministry of deliverance is about a boy from whom the apostles could not cast out a demon. In this case, Jesus says that *prayer* was the missing piece. It was the boy's father's unbelief that prevented the spirit from coming out. The prayer of the father, "Help my unbelief!" was a prayer of passion and honesty. He prayed for belief. Jesus shows here how the father did not think the demon could be cast out. We see this in Jesus's response to the boy's father, "If you can" is really calling the unbelief out. The unbelief of the father had prevented the apostles from even casting it out.

Jesus Heals a Boy Possessed by an Impure Spirit

When they came to the other disciples, they saw a large crowd around them and the teachers of the law arguing with them. As soon as all the people saw Jesus, they were overwhelmed with wonder and ran to greet him. "What are you arguing with them about?" he asked. A man in the crowd answered, "Teacher, I brought you my son, who is possessed by a spirit that has robbed him of speech. Whenever it seizes him, it throws him to the ground. He foams at the mouth, gnashes his teeth and becomes rigid. I asked your disciples to drive out the spirit, but they could not." "You unbelieving generation," Jesus replied, "how long shall I stay with you? How long shall I put up with you?

Bring the boy to me." So they brought him. When the spirit saw Jesus, it immediately threw the boy into a convulsion. He fell to the ground and rolled around, foaming at the mouth. Jesus asked the boy's father, "How long has he been like this?" "From childhood," he answered. "It has often thrown him into fire or water to kill him. But if you can do anything, take pity on us and help us." "'If you can'?" said Jesus. "Everything is possible for one who believes." Immediately the boy's father exclaimed, "I do believe; help me overcome my unbelief!" When Jesus saw that a crowd was running to the scene, he rebuked the impure spirit. "You deaf and mute spirit," he said, "I command you, come out of him and never enter him again." The spirit shrieked, convulsed him violently and came out. The boy looked so much like a corpse that many said, "He's dead." But Jesus took him by the hand and lifted him to his feet, and he stood up. After Jesus had gone indoors, his disciples asked him privately, "Why couldn't we drive it out?" He replied, "This kind can come out only by prayer." Mark 9:14-29

The boy's father had trouble believing because the boy had suffered from childhood. The father probably also feared the demon that possessed his son. Study this story and notice how Jesus got the boy's father to admit his unbelief. What happened right afterwards was that the boy was delivered immediately. But the boy looked like a corpse until Jesus touched the boy's hand and he arose. You will also note how Jesus commanded the spirit to never enter the boy again. This is a good "best practice" for any deliverance - that we make sure the spirits are commanded not to enter the person again.

In the gospel of Luke, this same story is repeated, but it also includes Jesus telling people about faith the size of a mustard seed. We must have faith in order to receive healing and freedom from impure spirits that come to make us blind, deaf, mute, and crippled. These are not God's will for us, but we have to have faith.

The next Bible account I'd like for us to study is found in the gospel of Matthew, chapter 8. In this account, Jesus heals a woman in bed with a fever by touching her hand. Then, that evening, people were brought to Him that were sick and tormented by demons. Notice how they were all delivered with "a word".

Jesus Heals Many

When Jesus came into Peter's house, he saw Peter's mother-in-law lying in bed with a fever. He touched her hand and the fever left her, and she got up and began to wait on him. When evening came, many who were demon-possessed were brought to him, and he drove out the spirits with a word and healed all the sick. This was to fulfill what was spoken through the prophet Isaiah: "He (Jesus) took up our infirmities and bore our diseases." Matthew 8:14-17

In most deliverance accounts described in the New Testament, Jesus used simple words and phrases like "Come Out!", or "Get Up and Walk!" simple commands that are filled with authority and power.

I want you to notice how, in almost every account "demon possessed" and "healed the sick" are always together. Demons do cause disease, so if someone has prayed healing for you and you have not received your healing, chances are, the demon must be cast out first before you can be healed; the demon is causing your sickness in the first place! Don't be scared by this; it is a beautiful thing to be delivered, and it is an incredible thing to witness as people are healed by the supernatural love of God.

This is what the Gospel is all about: restoring us to health and well-being. God made us in His image, as temples of His Holy Spirit; why would He want our bodies to be sick or partially useless? I don't believe it is God's will for people to be sick, crippled, or born with deformities. I believe it is the devil and demons that do these things and people have been blaming God for far too long. They aren't healed because they don't know Scripture, and even the ones that know Scripture don't have the faith to experience the miracles for themselves. They are living by their limited experiences instead of by faith in God's Word. It takes childlike faith to believe in these kinds of miracles and to go against what is generally accepted as normal. Now, injuries can happen naturally, and bodies do begin to break down with time, as we read in Biblical accounts. There are some things that are normal aging, and there are injuries that we bring upon ourselves. Jesus healed all of our infirmities and diseases just like the prophet Isaiah had predicted! We don't deserve to be punished for sin by getting sick. We are forgiven and free, and, according to Scripture, Jesus bore ALL our punishments for us. We have a clean record in God's eyes.

The gospel is all about Jesus paying for our sins, reuniting us with God, and giving us the inheritance of being a child of God. When we are fully forgiven, we are no longer under God's wrath and judgment. We are His people.

"Nevertheless, I will bring health and healing to it; I will heal my people and will let them enjoy abundant peace and security." Jeremiah 33:6

Jesus's ministry was all about restoration. God wants to heal His people and give them a good life. It is the enemy who wants you to suffer!

141

The final story we are going to cover is the account of the teacher in the church (or synagogue) who had a demon. Let's look at Luke, Chapter 4:

Jesus Drives Out an Impure Spirit

Then he went down to Capernaum, a town in Galilee, and on the Sabbath he taught the people. They were amazed at his teaching, because his words had authority. In the synagogue there was a man possessed by a demon, an impure spirit. He cried out at the top of his voice, "Go away! What do you want with us, Jesus of Nazareth? Have you come to destroy us? I know who you are—the Holy One of God!" "Be quiet!" Jesus said sternly. "Come out of him!" Then the demon threw the man down before them all and came out without injuring him. All the people were amazed and said to each other, "What words these are! With authority and power he gives orders to impure spirits and they come out!" And the news about him spread throughout the surrounding area. Luke 4:31-37

I want you to note that in this account, the demon told Jesus to "Go away!" It was afraid of Jesus! It knew its time was short and that Jesus had the power to destroy it. But Jesus did not respond to this demon, He just told it to be quiet and said "Come out of him!" Jesus gave a simple command that was filled with power and authority. The demon threw the man down, but it did come out without hurting the man.

Can you imagine if this happened at your church? What do you think would happen? Would you have the courage to help the man like Jesus did, or would you walk away? I want you to understand that since Jesus never sinned against God and only did the will of the Father, and we are supposed to imitate Jesus, then it just makes sense that as disciples, we are to do these things as well.

Jesus made deliverance and healing a central part of His ministry, and He gave us examples to show us how to walk in His same power. Do you think the demons were all expelled by the eleven disciples? Then why did the seventy get sent out? Did they get rid of every demon on earth? No, there are still demons that are tormenting people today, and we can't ignore this part of the Gospel.

Finding Faith - We don't need to be afraid of these things. We need to stop being ignorant and realize the possibilities here! Jesus gave His life and worked to make it possible for us to be free, and many are accepting mediocrity because we lack faith. If you can admit that you lack faith, that's a start, and I will tell you how to get the faith you are lacking. Romans Chapter 10 tells you exactly what to do, and I will personally testify that this is what worked for me.

Consequently, faith comes from hearing the message, and the message is heard through the word about Christ.
Romans 10:17

Faith comes by hearing the message about Christ, the testimony of the Gospel. Look up deliverance online and you'll hear story after story of people who were delivered and healed. If you don't believe me, keep searching. If you don't believe the Bible, keep searching. If you can't see the truth that is right in front of you, then pray for God to open your eyes! Maybe a demon is blinding your spiritual sight! You can be free, God can heal you, but He needs you to release His power by speaking to the demons and telling them to leave. You are the one (or if it is a generational thing, then it was your ancestors), who made deals with demons. I'm sick of watching demons torment my fellow brothers and sisters. I hope you get sick of them too, and use your God-given power to tell them to get lost! We don't want them anymore!

Do Not Focus on Demons - Demons are like germs and viruses; be healthy, and don't focus your energy "fighting" them. You might need to yell and scream at them when you are first learning to use your authority. But it isn't your personal power and authority that they obey; it is because you represent Jesus that they must listen to you. Yelling just tells them that you mean business. Once you know what you're doing, you can practice speaking calm, direct, and sternly because you will know your authority. You don't need to know everything about everything before you can cast out a devil. All you need to have is faith in God.

A good relationship with the Holy Spirit and hearing ears, along with a strong understanding of Scripture, will build your confidence and your faith. And I don't mean secondhand knowledge. You need to know Scripture for yourself. Eve had secondhand knowledge and look what happened to her! You've got to know God's Truth for yourself because you might doubt it if you just hear about it from me or anyone else.

Don't listen to anything the demons say, and if they try to speak to you and it scares you, just tell them to be silent. The last thing you need is to let fear creep in. You've got to focus on what God is telling you to do, not on the demon.

I have never been afraid of a demon the way I had assumed I would be before I had actually confronted one. People started coming to me for help because I desired to help God in this area. I knew when the person came, God sent them and I knew He would help me each step of the way.

I never imagined myself as someone who would "cast out a devil". I don't even like scary movies. If I can do this, you can do this. When I first began working in this area of ministry, God gave me a vision of myself in the Spirit, with grace and power like an angel, riding a lion. This lion represented Jesus, the Lion of the Tribe of Judah, and Jesus was attacking and biting the demons as I rode on His back and spoke the words that released freedom. He was my strength - He *is* my strength, and it doesn't matter how weak or insufficient I feel, Jesus is in me, and He is more powerful than the enemy who is at work in the world, waging war against the sons (and daughters) of God.

Then the dragon (Satan) was enraged at the woman and went off to wage war against the rest of her offspring—those who keep God's commands and hold fast their testimony about Jesus. Revelation 12:17

We will walk in this supernatural gift because we have a love for others. And if others are held down by the strongholds demons have built in their lives, we can't sit around and do nothing! Jesus commissioned ALL His followers to be a Holy Priesthood, to cast out demons, giving them power and authority to triumph over the enemy. We are promised success by God; it is our "heritage" as servants of God, our ABBA Father.

No weapon forged against you will prevail, and you will refute every tongue that accuses you. This is the heritage of the servants of the Lord, and this is their vindication from me," declares the Lord. Isaiah 54:17

Here is an example of this verse as a prayer:

No weapon formed against me shall prevail. I refute every tongue that accuses me. This is my heritage as a servant of the Lord, I am vindicated! Thus saith the Lord! Amen

You can take any verse in the Bible that applies to "you" or "them" when it's speaking to believers and turn it into a prayer with "I" or "me". This is an amazing way to use the Word of God as a sword to cut down the enemy and claim your victory and authority in Christ.

Even those that were not disciples of Jesus took authority and started casting out devils. The following verse was really interesting to me. It points out how a person, never trained by any of the disciples, or by Jesus, was able to cast out demons by simply using the authority of Jesus's name. It is also interesting how the disciples were telling him to stop! But Jesus rebuked His disciples, because anyone who associates themselves with Jesus, and goes up against the forces of darkness is for God, and God is for them! God rewards anyone who works to bring glory to the kingdom of light, even if all they do is get us a cup of water! Read the following message from the Book of Mark:

Whoever Is Not Against Us Is for Us

"Teacher," said John, "we saw someone driving out demons in your name and we told him to stop, because he was not one of us." "Do not stop him," Jesus said. "For no one who does a miracle in my name can in the next moment say anything bad about me, for whoever is not against us is for us. Truly I tell you, anyone who gives you a cup of water in my name because you belong to the Messiah will certainly not lose their reward. Mark 9:38-41

We can associate ourselves with Jesus by doing what Jesus did. For one person can say, "Lord, Lord," but Jesus says He never knew them, and another may not have met Jesus, but Jesus knows Him by his deeds. Are we for God or against Him? Do we try to do what Jesus did, or do we worry more about what other people think, instead of what God thinks? If you want to be a warrior for God, then you've got to take risks. Faith is spelled R-I-S-K. So go ahead and take a risk! A miracle and a great story of your own may be about to unfold. You never know what God will do, it might be amazing! Just as the religious rulers of Jesus's time denied these truths, so will many in today's time. But take heart!

However, as it is written: "What no eye has seen, what no ear has heard, and what no human mind has conceived" the things God has prepared for those who love him.
1 Corinthians 2:9

God has not revealed these mysteries to all believers. It is something we must seek to know and understand. Spiritual gifts are given to us because we seek them, so is authority over demons and sickness. To those that do not have this knowledge, it is foolishness to them; for it is only the Holy Spirit that makes sense of all this. To those that do not have understanding, all the teachings on demons are very frightening to them. All they know is what they see in the movies, or what they have read about. But you can't really understand how this works unless the Holy Spirit gives you discernment of spirits. The Israelites entered the wilderness selfish and grumbling, wandered for 40 years, and then died. Jesus entered the wilderness selfless and thankful, wandered for 40 days, and then emerged with power from the Holy Spirit to overcome the devil. God will test you to see if you are ready to receive power from the Holy Spirit so that you may do good works for God in this area of ministry. The only requirement on your part is willingness to listen to and obey God.

What we have received is not the spirit of the world, but the Spirit who is from God, so that we may understand what

God has freely given us. This is what we speak, not in words taught us by human wisdom but in words taught by the Spirit, explaining spiritual realities with Spirit-taught words. The person without the Spirit does not accept the things that come from the Spirit of God but considers them foolishness, and cannot understand them because they are discerned only through the Spirit. 1 Corinthians 2:12-14

I encourage you to say the following prayer to ask God for discernment of spirits if you do not think you have it already, or maybe you just want a deeper understanding. The only way to really understand this is to study, listen to testimonies, and to experience it for yourself. Once you become free, or you help someone else become free, you will be so excited and praise God! Then you'll see why the Gospel is such good news! You'll be jumping up in the morning, excited for what God is going to do through you to help people. It's an amazing life, and I pray that you will enjoy it to the fullest. Don't let anything stand in the way of spending time each day reading your Bible, praying, and living by God's rules. It's your life and God wants you to choose Him! There is nothing that compares to the sweetness of our Savior, the strength of His being, the abundance of His storehouses, the perfection of His healing, and the comfort of His grace. May God's Spirit be with you!

The only way to really understand this is to study, listen to testimonies, and to experience it for yourself.

Prayer to Receive the Gift of Discernment of Spirits

Father God, Thank You for making me Your child and giving me Your Holy Spirit. Please give me the gift of discerning of spirits so that I may do good works in Your Name, Jesus. Help me to see clearly and give me power to heal all diseases by Your authority, according to Luke, 6:19. Help increase my faith so that I may help others and glorify Your Name, Jesus. Amen!

CHAPTER 9

His Sheep Know His Voice

Therefore Jesus said again, "Very truly I tell you, I am the gate for the sheep. All who have come before me are thieves and robbers, but the sheep have not listened to them. I am the gate; whoever enters through me will be saved. They will come in and go out, and find pasture. The thief comes only to steal and kill and destroy; I have come that they may have life, and have it to the full.
John 10:7-10

Jesus tells us that His sheep know His voice, and they will not follow another. The only way to know whether or not it is Jesus's voice is to know Jesus. You know what your mother's voice sounds like, and there is no one that could imitate it, right? You just know. You know it because you've heard her voice millions of times, and you know her so well you would spot a fake right away. Even with currency (money), the way people are trained to spot a counterfeit is to have them study the real thing. If you know the real thing inside and out, you are able to spot a fake right away. It's the same with the Bible, if you know it inside and out, you'll know the voice of the enemy immediately.

Throughout your life, you'll want to make sure you are spending time in the Bible. The Bible is your sword, and without knowledge of it, you really have little knowledge of God. How can you conquer the enemy with a weapon in which you are unfamiliar? With study and prayer, you'll know exactly what God's

Truth is and what lies of demons are. Your goal is to know the voice of Jesus just like your own mother's voice. This book will do nothing for you if you do not seek guidance from the Holy Spirit and study your Bible. This book simply testifies that what the Bible says is true, and helps you develop your relationship with God. It also encourages you and helps you walk the way Jesus walked, full of love, light, power, and self-control.

Hearing the Voice of Jesus

The most important part of our faith is hearing from our Shepherd. We can memorize Scripture, volunteer our time, give our resources to God's work, and even be church leaders without following Jesus.

Hearing Jesus's voice is a gift from God, but we have to cultivate a hearing heart and apply ourselves to knowing Him. Throughout the Old and New Testaments there is a common theme that God tells His people, "Obey my voice, and I will be your God." Obeying God's voice is a most wonderful experience, and it becomes the central aspect through which your relationship with God resides. Your relationship with God comes through your heart, not through the mind or through the ears, or even through knowledge or faith. It comes through the heart and inclining one's ear to hear what God has to tell you. A "hearing heart" is critical in establishing and maintaining your relationship with Him. It is what distinguishes you as a true believer, and a follower of Jesus. The mark of a true disciple is quoted in the Book of John, 10:27. Jesus tells His disciples, "My sheep listen to my voice; I know them, and they follow me." Shepherds lead their sheep with their voice, and likewise, Jesus does the same. We cannot follow God if we cannot hear with our hearts. Pray regularly for God to give you a hearing heart!

Hearing the word of God produces faith. Hearing the Word can come in several forms. It could be through hearing a

151

sermon at church. It could be from hearing Scripture read. It could be from you reading your Bible. But Romans 10:17 is specifically referring to a word of God that is active and in the present tense, a word that is spoken right to your heart. When you are a new believer, this sounds like an abstract idea. As you learn to listen, God will speak more and more to you.

"Consequently, faith comes from hearing the message, and the message is heard through the word about Christ."
Romans 10:17

Your faith will grow as you *follow* His guidance and see the fruits thereof! You will see through your own personal experience that the word of God is trustworthy and true. And although you'll need to continue reading your Bible so that you can confirm what it is God wills for you, you will become more and more mature in Christ.

"We demolish arguments and every pretension that sets itself up against the knowledge of God, and we take captive every thought to make it obedient to Christ."
2 Corinthians 10:5

When we have learned to hear God's voice, the next step we take is to determine whether or not we want to follow what He says. I think this is the biggest reason people don't want to hear from God. They don't really want to know what He is going to say. It isn't that they don't want a relationship with Him; they just want it on their terms. As long as they can still watch football on Sunday, or go check out the cosmetics sale at the mall, they would be fine with having a relationship with God. But people assume that God would say "No" to these things, so they don't bother asking. They say, "Well, this day is just for me. I need a break. I deserve it. I've had a long week." So hearing from God just has to wait until tomorrow, and then they wonder why their life is, well, lifeless, boring, and full of strife.

Some people want a relationship with God, and they go to church, but they never hear His voice because they are too lazy to spend time with Him. They are moving forward but they aren't really sure where they are going. They've lost their bounce and really just pretend to be fulfilled when people ask: "How's the game? How are the kids? How's work?" Is that really all there is? I know because I was there. I was thirsty but nothing in this world really satisfied me. The truth was, I didn't really want to give my life totally to God when I first became a believer. I thought it was enough giving Him 90%. But that wasn't enough. I was afraid that if I gave Him everything - I mean total submission - He'd send me to a third world country to live in a tent with dirt and bugs to be a missionary. That was the last thing I wanted to do, so I just did what I thought He'd like me to do: what seemed nice, what seemed good and convenient to me. I did all kinds of volunteering. And it was great for a while, but it didn't last. Finally I got to the point where I almost lost everything, and that was when I really decided to give Him my life. That was the true day that Kelly Crumpley died. I humbled myself to God and He has blessed every area of my life. He healed me of all my physical problems (which were substantial), He successfully led me to help build an amazing marriage, He has blessed my children, He has blessed my finances, He has blessed me with amazing Christian friends, and that's just the beginning. I don't just believe what I am telling you, I have experienced God's faithfulness in my life. But it didn't happen until I was willing to incline my ear to God and listen to what He had to say! We can be saved and believe and be baptized but never listen to Him!

When people are really successful by the world's standards it is easy for them to get puffed up. God has to humble us in order to really work with us. Don't let what you assume God will do get in between you hearing from Him. After I submitted 100%, God reminded me that my dream as a little girl was to become a writer. My whole life I wanted to write but every time I tried to write I realized I didn't have anything to say! I believe that God put that dream in my heart, but I had to find Him in order to find my dream again. This book is a message about what God wants to say to His church, not about anything I have to say. The only good in me comes from Him!

"Take delight in the Lord, and he will give you the desires of your heart." Psalm 37:4

Jesus teaches about a hearing heart in Mark 4:9: "Then Jesus said, 'Whoever has ears to hear, let them hear.'" Jesus is obviously not talking about physical ears, since everyone there listening probably had them. He was speaking of hearing spiritually. God's lessons are spiritual lessons and they must be discerned through the Spirit.

Hearing the voice of God gives us daily direction and strength. Each day, we must choose to give the day to God. It is so easy to busy ourselves, and even burden ourselves with all the things we ought to get done. Or we don't do anything and just keep putting things off until we're so overwhelmed that we don't even know where to start. In all these circumstances, we can pray to God, whose door is open to us. What a privilege it is to enter His holy presence!

"Let us then approach God's throne of grace with confidence, so that we may receive mercy and find grace to help us in our time of need." Hebrews 4:16

In our time of need, God is always available to help us. God wants to help us! This is astonishing to me. The Creator of the universe cares about us so much that we can go to Him when we need help. That is really awesome. And I can testify that it's true. God is there, unlike anyone else, in our time of need. For me personally, I have experienced a peace that surpasses all understanding, just like Philippians 4:7, "And the peace of God, which transcends all understanding, will guard your hearts and your minds in Christ Jesus."

Instead of always trying to help ourselves, and improve ourselves, and all this self-help kind of stuff, all we need to do is come to know God. He can navigate us through even the most dreadful storms and bring us safely to shore. Even though a storm might be raging around us, if we are obedient to God, He will give us peace and a little glimmer of hope that we must press on. He wants us to let go of our control, and let Him be in control. We need to just scoot over, and let Him drive. It's really refreshing. And the great part is, He never gets lost. I might only see a little bit of the path, but He knows the whole way. As long as I stick with Him, it will be alright. God's special words to our hearts guide us on the path through the darkness.

"Your word is a lamp for my feet, a light on my path."
Psalm 119:105

CHAPTER 10

Prayer and Powerful Words

Prayer is a central part of a believer's life. All throughout the Bible we are encouraged to pray without ceasing, at all times, and for all things. Jesus told His disciples to think of Him as often as they eat and drink! The right to present our requests to God was won for us at the cross so that we may approach the throne in confidence. We enter His courts with praise and thanksgiving, knowing that our Father desires to hear us, and that He answers us promptly. We are given specific instructions on how to live a life of prayer:

Rejoice always, pray continually, give thanks in all circumstances; for this is God's will for you in Christ Jesus. 1 Thessalonians 5:17

Pray for Spiritual Gifts

We are told specifically to desire the spiritual gifts, which are received through prayer. These gifts allow us to supernaturally share God's love to others!

There are different kinds of gifts, but the same Spirit distributes them. There are different kinds of service, but the same Lord. There are different kinds of working, but in all of them and in everyone it is the same God at work.

Now to each one the manifestation of the Spirit is given for the common good. To one there is given through the Spirit a message of wisdom, to another a message of knowledge by means of the same Spirit, to another faith by the same Spirit, to another gifts of healing by that one Spirit, to another miraculous powers, to another prophecy, to another distinguishing between spirits, to another speaking in different kinds of tongues, and to still another the interpretation of tongues. All these are the work of one and the same Spirit, and he distributes them to each one, just as he determines. 1 Corinthians 12:4-11

God sends us spiritual gifts to help others and show them God's goodness and love. When I began seeking the spiritual gifts, I immediately started walking in them. I prayed to receive the gifts and for God to give me opportunities to use them to help others. God wants us to *eagerly desire* the spiritual gifts!

Now eagerly desire the greater gifts. 1 Corinthians 12:31

For example, when I began getting words of knowledge, I thought they were just my imagination. But when I didn't speak them, God would ask me why I didn't say the words He gave me. I was scared of how people would react, and worried that I would be wrong! Then I realized the doubt was not coming from God, but from the enemy. I was worried more about my reputation than I was about being obedient to God. After I repented, I asked God to give me another chance, and He did. I soon realized that it was more important that the person *hearing* the word knew what it meant, than for me to know what it meant.

Sometimes it would just be a single word, or maybe a number. Even when I've had lots of information, sometimes people still didn't get it. But then I started becoming more confident and people started receiving the message differently, and something started happening. Miracles began to occur and people were getting healed and set free! People started rededicating their lives to God and started experiencing the blessings of the Father. I'm so glad I stuck with it and didn't get discouraged! There wasn't anyone at my church doing this so I felt like a total weirdo. But God kept encouraging me and people were experiencing God's love. That was priceless!

Pray for Needs

God tells us that when we are in need, we should not be anxious about our situation, but we should pray to God. Through faith, we know that God will help us in our times of need.

"Do not be anxious about anything, but in every situation, by prayer and petition, with thanksgiving, present your requests to God." Philippians 4:6-7

The very next verse gives us a promise for what to expect when we pray, which really is worth more than all the gold in the world - it is the fruit of a strong prayer life and makes your whole world transform: "And the *peace of God*, which transcends all understanding, will guard your hearts and your minds in Christ Jesus." The peace of God is a complete, all-encompassing presence of God that just makes you feel good. It's really wonderful. During trials and miserable circumstances, through prayer, we are able to receive God's peace as a gift from Him.

The peace of God is a complete, all-encompassing presence of God that just makes you feel good.

To me, His peace is like the seal of confirmation to know that God heard me, and He's got me. I don't have to worry anymore. I still may need to listen for what He wants me to do about this or that. But I know in my spirit that God is in control, and even if it doesn't make any sense to me at the time, or I can't see the solution, God has got it handled. Anything I do at that point that isn't God-directed, is really just getting in God's way. It would be like me going to a mechanic and hiring him to fix my car, and then barging in and taking over the repairs. I still have to make the appointment, drive there, wait, and pick up my car. I just can't get in the way. I need to be involved in the process with God and engaged with finding the solution, not just sit back and expect God to fix everything. God can help us fix everything *if* we are willing to obey Him.

Prayer in the Spirit

Sometimes we don't know what to pray. I have experienced times when I am so upset that I can't even find the words. Other times, I am praying with a child and I know it's demonic but the last thing I want to do is scare them. These are perfect times for praying in tongues. When my son is sick, he asks me, "Pray in that *pretty voice*, Mommy." He wants me to sing in tongues over him! It comforts him, and I know that the Holy Spirit is giving me the words which perfectly meet our need. God brought this verse to my attention to confirm what He was leading me to do, and I have found this to be a great tool when I don't know what to say.

"When you are brought before synagogues, rulers and authorities, do not worry about how you will defend yourselves or what you will say, for the Holy Spirit will teach you at that time what you should say."
Luke 12:11-12

Inward Prayer

Our inward prayer life refers to our prayers that are focused on communion with God. It is the life-link between God and us. Without Him, we can do nothing, so this inward life is of vital importance. Our inward prayers deal with three main aspects, our speaking to God, our hearing from God, and our own introspection and evaluations of ourselves.

Inwardly speaking to God can be about anything at anytime. It can be confession, repenting, voicing a concern, asking for guidance, for repentance, for worship, and for knowledge. There are so many things we can talk to God about! We can talk to Him about anything at anytime. Hearing from God is often just quieting ourselves and letting God lead our day. "What do you want me to do today, Lord?" or, "What do I do next?"

Intercessory Prayer

We can talk to God on behalf of someone else; we call this *intercession*. Each person has to work out their own salvation, but we can always pray for God to reveal things to people and work in their lives. If it is His will, He will do it. God can reveal anything to anyone, believer or unbeliever, because He is God. This may end up being a step for them towards building their own relationship with God. Intercessory prayer is usually for unbelievers who can not enter into God's presence and make the requests themselves. It could also be for new believers that aren't sure what to say. It could be that we are praying for healing or protection for someone; this is *interceding* for them. We can also pray for our schools, law enforcement, politicians, governments, and more. We can talk to God about anyone or anything we want.

When we are first saved, Jesus is our intercessor. Once we are baptized in water and with the Holy Spirit and fire of God, we can approach the throne confidently and make requests for others.

Let us then approach God's throne of grace with confidence, so that we may receive mercy and find grace to help us in our time of need. Hebrews 4:16

Hearing from God

Hearing from God is a skill that requires practicing quieting ourselves and softening our hearts to hear His voice. We need to come before Him with clean hearts and a clean conscience. We must be humble, repenting of even our unknown sins, and be consciously aware of His majesty and holiness. We also need to be aware of our own righteousness which stands solely on Jesus's work of atonement. When we know we are clean and sanctified, we know that God will talk to us; or at least that we won't be destroyed in His Presence! When we hear from God, we also need to know Scripture so that we can verify what is said. Sometimes the enemy will come as an angel of light and deceive us to think we are hearing from God when it is really a demon. When we know God's Word we are able to spot the fake right away, and are still wise to verify that our word from God is in alignment with Scripture. Romans 12:2 tells us to renew our minds, so that we may test and approve God's perfect will.

Do not conform to the pattern of this world, but be transformed by the renewing of your mind. Then you will be able to test and approve what God's will is—his good, pleasing and perfect will. Romans 12:2

Renewing our minds means learning everything from God's Word, the Tree of Life, and not touching the Tree of Knowledge of Good and Evil, which is the flesh and worldly wisdom. Only when we believe God do we experience the peace, provision, health, and abundant life that God has planned for us.

I have found that in the beginning, God only shows us compassion, love, peace, and acceptance. But we still may sin and hold parts of our life to ourselves, not completely submitted to Him. We may not become the "new man" that Christ describes, and, therefore, we may still struggle with the same problems that brought us to our knees in the first place. That is why it's so important to read the Bible and seek to hear God's voice. God will guide us on a path that resembles the story in Exodus. We will be walking a path that many have walked before. We will become like clay in the potters hands and will seek fellowship with God and with other believers. The Holy Spirit in us will guide the way.

As we mature, God will show us parts of ourselves that need refining. Once we accept them, God will give us the opportunity to "field test" our refined skill. For example, when I used to get sick, I would make a big huge deal about it, be a big baby, and get mad if people didn't dote over me. I acted completely helpless and tried to milk it for everything I could. Not on purpose, it's just something I learned growing up. When I became a follower of Christ, I realized this was totally twisted and selfish, and I prayed for God to help me act uprightly! I didn't realize I would need to field test this, so sure enough I got some bad burns on my hand from baking I couldn't use my left hand for 2-3 weeks.

In the past, I would have had a big fit. But instead, I was able to pray for God to remove the pain, which He did! I had zero pain after praying twice. Actually, the second prayer was more like a command to my hand for the spirit of pain to leave. So even though I couldn't use my left hand, I still felt great and was almost totally functional. And I didn't need to ask for help with my chores, for God put it on my daughter's heart to help me and offer help to me often! I was so blessed and overcome with God's love towards me, and the love of my family; I couldn't believe it.

Before, I used to expect help from others when I was sick or injured and NEVER got it. Now, I just pray to God, lifting everything up to Him, thankful for Him, knowing that He works all things for my good, and the help just comes without my effort or worry at all. It is such a transformation to live by faith in God. I just knew He would help me. The example I'm setting for my children is so much better now that I am a believer, and I am so thankful! I'd hate for them to have copied my old behavior of trying to manipulate people. Parents, our children copy everything we do! I hope also that you will do a little introspection of your own, and ask God to reveal something to you that you can then "field test" your faith. I also pray that you will pass with flying colors! You will be so happy you did!

Power of the Spoken Word

God spoke the world into existence. The spoken word can bring blessings, or it can bring curses. Words can bring healing, or they can bring pain. It can make demons leave, or it can invite them in. Our words should always glorify God, and be filled with truth and love. God tells us to study His words and to keep them in our hearts, to meditate on them, for they are life to us and provide healing.

Fix these words of mine in your hearts and minds; tie them as symbols on your hands and bind them on your foreheads.
Deuteronomy 11:18

God tells us over and over again to listen to God's Word and keep them in our hearts. For what is in the heart will come out of our mouths! Our spoken words are an overflow from our hearts, which is why we need a discerning heart. We need to read, savor, chew, swallow, and digest God's word so it becomes who we are. It is life and renewal for our bodies! God's Word is spiritual food and it strengthens the Holy Spirit within us. We can speak God's Word over our lives and bring the truth of His will over us.

My son, pay attention to what I say;
turn your ear to my words.
Do not let them out of your sight,
keep them within your heart;
for they are life to those who find them
and health to one's whole body.
Above all else, guard your heart,
for everything you do flows from it.
Keep your mouth free of perversity;
keep corrupt talk far from your lips.
Let your eyes look straight ahead;
fix your gaze directly before you.
Give careful thought to the paths for your feet
and be steadfast in all your ways.
Do not turn to the right or the left;
keep your foot from evil.
Proverbs 4:20-27

In God's Kingdom are life, healing, and abundance. The enemy would like you to think otherwise. God has a perfect plan for us, but in order for us to experience it, we must declare it! God spoke the world into existence and that is our basis for using words to create our reality.

I knew that God wanted me to write, but I had no idea how that was going to work. The demons were making me think, "I have responsibilities; I have work to do. I can't just spend all my time researching and praying and writing! That will never happen. If I talk about spiritual warfare people will think I am crazy. I have to make money. Most writers don't make a dime." But God told me something different. He said, "Trust me and follow me with all your heart. All the provisions will be made for you. All you need to do is take the first step in faith." So that is what I decided to do. I also declared that I was an author, and that I was a teacher of God's Word. I told everybody! And money came in that just didn't make sense to me, but God had it all figured out. I just needed to believe He would take care of me, and He did! He became everything to me, and I have never looked back! I told the devil to take his hands off my money and off each member of my family. "Devil, in the Name of Jesus, I break your power over my (finances, health condition, influence, specific person, etc.)!"

The enemy reared up pretty hard as I was writing this book. He knew he was defeated, and he was trying every last thing to try and get me off track. But I stayed submitted to God and stood on the rock as the waves crashed around me. I focused on God, and the words I spoke were words of *victory* and *life* over the situation, even though my thoughts were bombarded with discouragement.

The tongue has the power of life and death, and those who love it will eat its fruit. Proverbs 18:21

CHAPTER 11

Perfect Faith

Having perfect faith means that we absolutely know for sure what God says. That means we need to press in and read the Bible to discover the blessings of the Father. I can tell you what it says and testify that it has proven true for me, but you need to grow your own faith. As I have said before, faith comes by hearing. Let me remind of you of this verse again:

Consequently, faith comes from hearing the message, and the message is heard through the word about Christ.
Romans 10:17

God wants you to know His Word and study it. I have watched the New Testament come to life before my very eyes, and I wouldn't trade it for anything. As you read the Bible, you'll start to see it manifest in your own life. Jesus is the Word of God in the flesh. He is the living Word.

The Word became flesh and made his dwelling among us. We have seen his glory, the glory of the one and only Son, who came from the Father, full of grace and truth.
John 1:14

Believing that you are truly forgiven, and standing on that truth is the key to your faith. Visiting your past, apart from the blood of Jesus can be dangerous. I have stated this in more ways than one throughout this book. It is essential that we know who we are in Christ, and once we do, we need to share that gift with others. There is nothing better than looking in someone's eyes when the light bulb goes on the scales fall from their eyes (Acts 9:18), when they realize who they are in Christ and that they don't need to be afraid anymore. There is a boldness that comes when you receive the Holy Spirit.

That one person will go on and influence their family, their co-workers, and even their own church. Faith grows when we share our testimonies of Jesus and encourage each other in love and truth. I love how God loves us and never gives up on us. I'd have given up on me a long time ago! There has been much joy in my journey, but there has also been sorrow. I have been persecuted and I'm sure there will be more. In fact, I'm proud to be persecuted, because it means I'm ticking the devil off! I love watching as people realize how their life doesn't align with God, and then watching them make the decision to truly repent. It is absolutely amazing to watch God change people's lives and exalt them after they humble themselves to Him.

Faith grows when we share our testimonies of Jesus and encourage each other in love and truth.

Here is a story about a woman who was delivered and went on to praise God and become born-again. This story happened at our annual women's retreat. I was on the prayer team, and I was downstairs praying with a woman when my roommate ran to get me. She said God told her to come get me because He wanted me to go upstairs and pray for a certain woman. So I finished up and went upstairs. When I walked into the room, there was a woman laying face down on the floor, and there were about 10 people praying for her. Some were crying. They had been there for some time. I asked God what He wanted me to do. He told me to go over and lay my hands on her. Then He told me that she had a spirit of infirmity and that I needed to cast it out. So very quietly, I told it to come out. Then I said, "Let her go!" Immediately the spirit left.

Then I asked God what to do next. He told me to command her pain to leave and for her back to be healed, so I did. Then I told her to get up and check her back. So she stood up and wiggled all around trying to see if she had pain. She was free! The look of relief on her face was wonderful! She flung open the double doors on the balcony and said, "Praise God! Jesus healed my back! I'm healed! I'm healed!" We were crying tears of joy! Then she hugged me and told me that she had been in severe pain, had gone through back surgery, and had crawled up to the prayer room. I believe she wanted to be healed that day. She had faith in God prior to that point but she needed someone who knew their authority to *exercise* their authority over the spirit. God wasn't denying her healing, but until the spirit was commanded to leave, she couldn't be healed. God gave us the authority and also the *responsibility* to heal sickness and disease as well. He works miracles through us. Our words release His power and what we ask, He will give us.

God wasn't denying her healing, but until the spirit was commanded to leave, she couldn't be healed.

In that day you will no longer ask me anything. Very truly I tell you, my Father will give you whatever you ask in my name. Until now you have not asked for anything in my name. Ask and you will receive, and your joy will be complete. John 16:23-24

A better translation from the original Greek for the word translated as "ask" is "demand". When we are praying God's will over our life or someone else's life, God promises to do what He says. He made a blood covenant with us. He has made us so many promises that we are yet to discover! He has given us authority to have victory over the devil and wants us to live life abundantly. I have experienced amazing things and you can too!

When you ask, you do not receive, because you ask with wrong motives, that you may spend what you get on your pleasures. James 4:3

When you are asking for things that glorify God and His Kingdom, you will be blessed. When you pray in alignment with God's Word, and know your relationship with Him in Christ, as His beloved bride, you will lack no good thing. What perfect husband would deny his perfect wife the things she desires?

Therefore, since we are surrounded by such a great cloud of witnesses, let us throw off everything that hinders and the sin that so easily entangles. And let us run with perseverance the race marked out for us, fixing our eyes on Jesus, the pioneer and perfecter of faith. For the joy set before him he endured the cross, scorning its shame, and sat down at the right hand of the throne of God. Consider him who endured such opposition from sinners, so that you will not grow weary and lose heart. Hebrews 12:1-3

Jesus is the perfecter of our faith. We can study Him and His ministry and see that His whole purpose was to show us the way to live a victorious, healthy, abundant, outward lifestyle. His purpose was to ruin the works of the devil, and to clean our conscience of dead works so we can walk in His righteousness. He healed the sick, cast out devils, and made disciples; we should imitate Him.

Living in this world, we are bombarded by the lies of the enemy. But God's Truth brings life and healing. Here's a list of a few lies along with God's Truth to set you straight:

SATAN'S LIES - God's Truth

1. Satan says, "You're too bad; you can never be saved."

"God says, "Though your sins are like scarlet, they shall be as white as snow; though they are red as crimson, they shall be like wool." (Isaiah 1:18)

2. Satan says, "If you were saved, you wouldn't do the things you do."

God says, "Indeed, there is no one on earth who is righteous, no one who does what is right and never sins." (Ecclesiastes 7:20)

3. Satan says, "You've sinned too often; God won't forgive you."

God says, "If we confess our sins, he is faithful and just and will forgive us our sins and purify us from all unrighteousness." (1 John 1:9)

4. Satan says, "You're finished. You may as will give up."

God says, "Being confident of this, that he who began a good work in you will carry it on to completion until the day of Christ Jesus." (Philippians 1:6)

5. Satan says, "God can't use you."

God says, "For we are God's handiwork, created in Christ Jesus to do good works, which God prepared in advance for us to do." (Ephesians 2:10)

6. Satan says, "You'll never make it."

God says, "I can do all this through him who gives me strength." (Philippians 4:13)

7. Satan says, "The situation is hopeless."

God says, "Anyone who is among the living has hope—even a live dog is better off than a dead lion!" (Ecclesiastes 9:4)

8. Satan says, "Things will never be good again."

God says, "Why, my soul, are you downcast? Why so disturbed within me? Put your hope in God, for I will yet praise him, my Savior and my God." (Psalm 42:5)

9. Satan says, "The obstacles are too great."

God says, "I am the Lord, the God of all mankind. Is anything too hard for me?" (Jeremiah 32:27)

10. Satan says, "You always have failed, and you always will fail."

God says, "But thanks be to God! He gives us the victory through our Lord Jesus Christ." (1 Corinthians 15:57)

11. Satan says, "You're washed up."

God says, "But you were washed, you were sanctified, you were justified in the name of the Lord Jesus Christ and by the Spirit of our God." (1 Corinthians 6:11)

I would like you to take a moment and reflect on some of the lies that you may still be holding on to. Take out a clean sheet of paper and write them down. After you've you're your list, go to BibleGateway.com. In the "search" field, type some of the key words from your list. See if any Scriptures come up that pertain to your specific beliefs. Anything that is on your list could be exploited by the enemy, and used to make you feel separated from God. You can overcome the enemy by resting on God's Truth. Jesus gives us freedom, peace, and strength in Him. Don't let anything separate you from the love of God. He was willing to pay such a high price to save you from death; He gave the life of His own Son to save YOU.

In him was life, and that life was the light of all mankind.
John 1:4

There are so many promises of God's goodness hidden within the Bible, I encourage you to discover them on your own. We shouldn't just read the Bible, but we should live it, and then our faith will grow. We can't get faith without *experiencing* what the Word of God says. But how can we experience and expect something that we know nothing about? We can't grow our faith until we cultivate a relationship with the Father and realize we are adopted into His magnificent Kingdom through faith in His Son Jesus Christ, Yeshua Hamashiach. The Bible comes to life when

172

you know the Holy Spirit. You will become totally enthralled with its beauty and power.

As you watch lives around you transform, be careful to realize that it is Jesus working *through* you, otherwise power can puff you up and ruin your character. Focus on cultivating your relationship with God. Read your Bible and spend time in fellowship with other believers. Remain a humble servant.

Don't be afraid of the enemy. I have NEVER been afraid of demons, and I'm not exactly what you would call a brave or hearty individual. I'm 5 feet 4 inches, and 120 lbs. I know it's Christ in me who is strong so I don't need to be. I just have to have faith in my God! Pray, worship, and spend time listening to what God says to *you* through the Holy Spirit. In time, you will fall in love with God just as I did, and be seated with Christ in heavenly places. You will, one day, see yourself as His bride, perfectly united in spirit, mind, and body.

> *As you watch lives around you transform, be careful to realize that it is Jesus working through you, otherwise power can puff you up and ruin your character.*

CHAPTER 12

Walking in Authority

In order to walk with authority you need to know your identity in Christ. You have to die to yourself, be buried with Him, and be raised again to the newness of life. This is the empowered, Holy Spirit led life. If you aren't sure if you've been born again, you probably haven't! All the authority and spiritual gifts you need belong to the Holy Spirit. If you pray and ask God to lead you and fill you with His Spirit, He will. This "filling" and empowering is something I pray for all the time. I am constantly asking God for more of His Spirit. "More God, more!" I ask Him. I know that I can do nothing on my own. I also have made the decision to let God use me as an instrument of righteousness in order to help others. I began by allowing extra time when I would go shopping in case God wants to use me. God was using me so much that my daughter started bringing a book with her when she would go out with me! I began getting words of knowledge, and I let God lead me to those who wanted prayer. I saw lots of people healed, and those that didn't immediately see results at least felt loved. It's amazing what God will do with a person who is open to His leading.

Prayer and evangelism without the Holy Spirit can be offensive. I can always tell when someone has the Holy Spirit, and I love it when they pray for me. I can also tell when someone is just doing good works in the flesh- I don't care for those prayers too much. They always seem to be empty and demeaning. You've got to seek God's Holy Spirit to become a true light to others.

You can't take something that is corrupted and make it uncorrupted. You have to become a new creation. Take a piece of fruit for example: once it starts to rot, there's nothing that will make it stop rotting away. You can't take the corruptible and make it incorruptible. You need to be born of God, with the incorruptible seed of His Spirit. When you are "born again," the old self passes away, and we become new *in Christ*. Jesus explains it like this:

"No one sews a patch of unshrunk cloth on an old garment. Otherwise, the new piece will pull away from the old, making the tear worse. And no one pours new wine into old wineskins. Otherwise, the wine will burst the skins, and both the wine and the wineskins will be ruined. No, they pour new wine into new wineskins."
Mark 2:21-22

You can't just work on making yourself better. That is a psychology mindset of self-improvement, which relies on your own power, and not the power of God. There is a difference between maturing in faith, and using Jesus as a moral example of character improvements. Character improvements are good, but they don't make you a Christian. If you become born again, however, you will have true, lasting character change borne out of maturing in faith. Without faith and the supernatural help of God, our efforts of self improvement will be in vain - our energy will be used up. By dying to ourselves, and being made alive in Christ, we can tap into unlimited resources. Jesus tells us:

"Whoever finds their life will lose it, and whoever loses their life for my sake will find it." Matthew 10:39

And Jesus goes on to say:

"And everyone who has left houses or brothers or sisters or father or mother or wife or children or fields for my sake will receive a hundred times as much and will inherit eternal life." Matthew 19:29

Surrendering to God is a hard thing to do. It takes complete humility to give everything to Him, sometimes not even knowing Him or His word to know that He promises you goodness. But we cannot experience intimate fellowship with God until we surrender to Him and put Him first in our lives. Anything that we refuse to give up becomes an idol to us and creates a barrier between us and God. What Jesus is trying to tell us through the cross is that without bringing ourselves to the cross, we cannot inherit eternal life. Just believing that Jesus is the Savior isn't enough, even demons know that. It is us coming alongside Christ and following His divine command in our lives that makes us His. It is us turning our ear to Him, turning our minds from the culture of the world into knowing God's Word and understanding His will.

There is life in dying to ourselves and all the passions of the flesh and living new by the Spirit of God. There is freedom and peace and joy! It's hardly a sacrifice at all! All the things I needed to give up were replaced by WAY better things. I will testify personally to this truth. When I surrendered to God and was willing to give everything up is when I really started to live. Everything inside was made light and all the broken pieces were mended. Memories still lingered, but all the pain of my past was gone. Then over a period of a few months, all of my bodily problems were healed, including psychological, emotional, and ALL physical injuries. Financially, I was blessed, and with no extra effort, everything I had became beautiful and blessed by God. My outlook on my life was focused on God (not on myself), and so

He blessed me. I appreciated every little thing and the things started multiplying. The quality of my life improved so much it could only be because of Him. Relationships were restored because of God's love filling me and I was able to overflow with love for other people who had previously caused me unrest.

All God asks is for us to trust Him and be obedient to Him. But it is so hard! It's so hard, especially, to trust after you've been hurt and let down by people. But as you begin to build a relationship with God, you learn more and more that you can trust Him, and that His ways are always best! I promise you, He will NEVER lead you astray! The best way to be an "overcomer" is to balance intimate fellowship with God and awareness of how the enemy is working to knock you down.

For everyone born of God overcomes the world. This is the victory that has overcome the world, even our faith. Who is it that overcomes the world? Only the one who believes that Jesus is the Son of God. 1 John 5:4-5

To be an "overcomer" also means to keep praying even though you don't see instant results. Developing perseverance is hard to do, but, it's a miracle working practice! In the Book of Daniel, in Chapter 10, we read how "praying through" was essential to Daniel's success. I encourage you to stop and read Chapter 10, verses 1-21. Daniel receives a vision about a great war, prays, and then fasts from choice foods, wine, and lotions for three weeks. Then Daniel is visited by an angel - it is obviously not a human based on the description - with a body like topaz, and a face like lightening. This was one of God's messengers, an angel that is loyal to God. The angel tells Daniel that he is "highly esteemed" and that God saw that Daniel had humbled himself and set his mind to understanding, so God sent the angel to answer Daniel's prayer. How awesome it would be to hear that you are highly esteemed by God!

Again the one who looked like a man touched me and gave me strength. "Do not be afraid, you who are highly esteemed," he said. "Peace! Be strong now; be strong."
Daniel 10:18-19

The next part is where it gets even more interesting, the angel then explains how the "Prince of Persia" detained him for three weeks from delivering the answer to God's prayer. And furthermore, that the angel will also be detained on His way back to God's throne. There was a spiritual battle that took place between the angel of God, and the demon that had dominion over Persia. Because of this battle, Daniel's answer to his prayer was delayed.

It is good for us to humble ourselves to God by fasting and praying, but it is even better to repent and put on the mind of Christ, with immediate access to God's presence through the Holy Spirit. It's the same as if there were snail mail in Daniel's day, but in current times, we can just send God a text to release the troops. Daniel's prayer had a major impact on his society during that day, and we can have an even bigger impact on ours if we keep our minds on the things of God, and use the authority Jesus has purchased for us.

We can be commanding officers and leaders in God's army if we take up the responsibility. We can take back cities that are filled with sin and violence. We can bind up spirits that are over evil businesses and schools, all we have to do is grab on to God's promises and stand firm on the Word of God! Let us have more power over the enemy than he has against us. Let us be watchful of him and not be ignorant of his devices.

Be alert and of sober mind. Your enemy the devil prowls around like a roaring lion looking for someone to devour.
1 Peter 5:8

In the <u>Art of War</u> by Sun Tzu, one tactic that is used by an enemy is the element of surprise. Your enemy hides all their movements from you; then they look for a moment of weakness and launch their attack. The enemy of our souls (Satan) loves to use this tactic by making you think that demons don't exist or that they don't bother people.

Another tactic used in war times is to cut off all resources to an enemy to weaken them or drive them out. This can be cutting off their food supply or their ability to forge weapons. Now, the demons use this tactic against us by cutting us off from God and luring us away into other activities. They can distract us with illnesses, "things to do," and "worldly stuff" that we don't really need. What I am suggesting is that you use the following weapons against them.

Here's how it works: let's say you have a demon of anger, and every time something happens, it whispers in your ear, "Look, they did it again! Those idiots! You aren't going to let them get away with that are you? You've got to get back at them! They deserve it anyway; look what they did to you! They probably did it on purpose!" It goes on and on. This demon is trying to get you to become angry because it *feeds* off your anger. So if you cut off its food supply and starve it out by not entertaining these thoughts, instead, lifting up that person in prayer, releasing them into God's loving hands, and praying for guidance, this demon has no power over you. The only power that demon had was because you gave it to him. You entertained the thoughts it put into your head, and every time

The only power that demon had was because you gave it to him.

179

something happened that could be twisted; it twisted the situation with the hopes of making you angry.

This can be the same with any kind of demon. If you make deals with them by believing their lies, they become more and more attached to you, kind of like a parasite. They are feeding off your negative energies, lusts, and ungodly behaviors. This is especially true with demons that make you crave unhealthy foods and, in turn, feed off the guilt and shame you feel after eating. Remember, demons are persons without bodies, and they are very warped with extreme appetites for sin. They want you to sin in order to gratify their desires.

Let's say a demon of suicide is bothering you; it wants you to kill yourself. It will whisper in your ear horrible thoughts until you feel like nothing and even try and tell you that the world would probably just be a better place without you.

The minute you start agreeing with it, its attachment to you grows. It's hooked you. Now, you still haven't committed suicide, but it keeps pushing. It makes you think you are hopeless and unworthy of God's mercy and grace. It slowly breaks you down inside, dragging you further and further away from God. This could also happen with a demon of murder, theft, lying, adultery, homosexuality, rage, etc. You may have never acted on its probing thoughts, but you wonder where those thoughts came from. You didn't think them up – people don't think like that. God didn't make us to think like that. It isn't normal – it's a demon!

We've got to stop listening to these parasites and cast them to the pit where they belong! Stop putting up with it, and just reject those thoughts. If it isn't a godly thought, don't listen to it! Don't let any un-Godly thoughts "land"!

We demolish arguments and every pretension that sets itself up against the knowledge of God, and we take captive every thought to make it obedient to Christ. 2 Corinthians 10:5

God always acts in love and truth. Love can be twisted without God's truth, and truth can be twisted without God's love. So be on your guard, and make sure you know what Scripture really says and means! All you have to do is ask God for discernment whenever you hear a voice you recognize or suspect as demonic. Then you can just tell it to leave, just like you would anyone else – "In the Name of Jesus, I command you to leave right now. I reject those thoughts and renounce any connection you have to me. You have no right to be here, leave me now." It's really simple, and Jesus had an even simpler method, usually just, "Come out of him!"

It's not really a set of certain words that makes the difference; it's just you taking the authority that Jesus has given you already and exercising that authority. It's all about your attitude. Do you really want it to go away? Then just tell it to leave! The longer you wait, the more attached it will become, and the more it will make you think it's too late. It's never too late, and its roots are never too deep to be removed from you. If you need help, just pray for the Holy Spirit's guidance. You can be delivered.

> *It's not really a set of certain words that makes the difference; it's just you taking the authority that Jesus has given you already and exercising that authority.*

God created you to be a light, and demons are like little mud balls that attach themselves to your light-filled spirit and block out the light. They feed on your negative energy, and the mud ball grows until all your light is covered. The light is still inside you, but it's blocked. When you align yourself with God's Spirit and His divine energy of love, these negative demons and energies can't survive. Sometimes it is hard to remove them, just like if you step in the mud and let it dry on your shoe. It makes it harder to clean off because it's stuck in the grooves in the bottom. You have to be a little more forceful with your scrubbing. Maybe even get out the soap and a scrub brush. But when you wash the mud off right away, it washes away easily and it doesn't have time to adhere to your shoe. Your clean shoe is under there somewhere, you've just got to find it! Get out the Word of God and be washed spiritually with the renewing of your mind: that you are made to be free of these impure spirits!

God's Holy and pure light-filled spirit is within you. God made you exactly the way He wanted you; you are beautiful and magnificent in Christ. No one is made by accident, each person has somewhere around a one-in-a-trillion chance of being born, so the fact that YOU exist is a miracle in itself. God made us to reign on the earth, and we are also seated spiritually with Christ in heavenly places.

Are you sick? Pray in the Spirit for eyes to see the source and pray accordingly. Speak to your body and command it to be healed! Tell any impure spirits to come out and command your body to be healed.

God gave us the Holy Spirit which enables us to do all things. Jesus refers to the Holy Spirit as The Comforter, knowing full well that we are going to have times that we are very uncomfortable! Don't forget that God's Holy Spirit is in you which is the same Spirit that raised Jesus from the dead and healed His wounds. Every miracle that Jesus did, you can also do because it is the same Spirit within you. In fact, Jesus commands you to do it.

*Heal the sick, raise the dead, cleanse those who have leprosy,
drive out demons. Freely you have received; freely give.*
Matthew 10:8

Jesus says that these signs will follow those who believe.
Are you sick? Pray in the Spirit for eyes to see the source and pray
accordingly. Speak to your body and command it to be healed!
Tell any impure spirits to come out and command your body to
be healed. It is really not hard to do. If you can talk, you can make
it happen, for God's Holy Spirit does the work, and you are just
releasing its power through the power of the spoken word. Let
your tongue and your entire body be an instrument of
righteousness, a vessel that the Holy Spirit uses to let the light
shine in others.

Spiritual warfare is all about seeing the beauty and light that
God created and helping it emerge. It's about washing away all the
mud and grime that has attached itself to you, spiritually, and
walking in the light. It's about seeing that light within others, too,
seeing past their anger and frustration and bad behavior and
finding out the root of their troubles. It's about helping them to
see things from a spiritual position, from heaven, and from the
cross. It's about living from that place of perfect peace and love,
and not entertaining the enemy. The enemy is a liar.

You were created to be victorious. All the tools you need
are in your Bible, the Living Word of God, and all wisdom and
spiritual gifts are available through the Holy Spirit. God gives all
this to you freely. It's so easily accessible that many people look
past it and don't realize the treasure that they have been given.
That Bible may be sitting on a shelf, not touched for days, months,
even years. I am urging you to keep watch, fellow brothers and
sisters, to awaken from your slumber and come out of the
darkness and into the light of life, where there is peace, joy, love,
and abundant life!

Knowing the Holy Spirit and relying on His divine guidance along the way is so crucial. Devoting yourself to prayer and developing a strong inner prayer life will be your best-spent time because it's time you spend getting to know your Heavenly Father. My desire for you is that you will become free and be filled with God's love, and develop into a cup that is overflowing to help others. Your desire to help others should be out of love for people, and never for your own glory. I have to admit it is quite exhilarating to find out that you have authority over impure spirits, and the authority to heal ALL diseases. When the seventy-two disciples came back to Jesus, they were excited that the demons submitted to them, too! (Luke 10:17) Keep in mind, it is not our own power at work; it is always Him. God should always be our focus, our center, our rock. He is the vine, and we are the branches. We never want to be disconnected from the vine or else we will wither.

I am the vine; you are the branches. If you remain in me and I in you, you will bear much fruit; apart from me you can do nothing. John 15:5

We are ALL called to be light. As we walk with our God, turning our ears to Him and praying for pure hearts that serve Him, our flame will burn brighter and brighter. The world has many ways to lure us away from Jesus, and to make us follow the wrong path. Maybe even a good path, but not the narrow path. That is why YOUR personal relationship with Jesus is so important - if you don't know the voice of your Shepherd, you won't know where to go. Shepherds lead with their voice. They don't force sheep to do anything, and sheep don't attack. The shepherd keeps the sheep safe as long as they are in the fold. But if the sheep wander away, they are at risk. We all wander from time to time, and Jesus always comes after us and tries to bring us back. But ultimately it is our choice to obey the voice of our

184

Shepherd, sometimes even letting Him carry us if we are too weak to walk by ourselves.

Stay inside the house of God, following the Shepherd's voice, and you will be okay. This is why you need to read and study God's Word: so you may be able to verify the truth of the voice you hear speaking to your heart by testing it against the personality of the Spirit of God that is revealed in the Bible. The enemy knows the word of God, too, and he tries to twist it and make the meaning very different than what God intends. It is our responsibility to read the Bible for ourselves, every day if possible, and make sure we are fresh and on track.

The Holy Spirit must rule over our flesh, meaning that we need to feed it, even as we feed our physical bodies food. The Bible is spiritual food, and it is just as important as eating actual food. Fasting is so helpful in training the Spirit to rule over our flesh. Fasting takes our mind off the physical and lets us focus spiritually. Refraining from food, even for a few hours, will help us focus on a particular prayer and can bring amazing results. The inner spiritual life is something that is grown over time, and hearing God's Voice is part of that. It is intertwined; one without the other makes us weak. We need to spend time in prayer and also in listening to God for His advice, comfort, encouragement, and direction.

We can also spend this time receiving visions and prophetic words, depending on the need. All spiritual gifts are available from the Holy Spirit, and as we need them to help others, we will receive them if we develop our spiritual senses. We are each given God's Holy Spirit as a gift, and as a seal that we are His: accepted children of the Most High God.

Our Heavenly Father can give us any gift He chooses through His Spirit, and at any time. These gifts can be healing, words of knowledge, speaking in other tongues, prophecy, and more. All these supernatural gifts are available to any of us when we need them! No one owns a particular gift; it is always the Holy

Spirit who is enabling us to perform these gifts. Maybe you think that only great people can walk in these supernatural gifts. The reality is, God can use ordinary people to do extraordinary things. It is our job however, to spend time in prayer, asking for these gifts, and opening our eyes to the world, looking for ways to help. God will lead us (if we are listening!); we need not push things on others, but just let it flow and let the Holy Spirit guide us in all good works.

Now to each one the manifestation of the Spirit is given for the common good. To one there is given through the Spirit a message of wisdom, to another a message of knowledge by means of the same Spirit, to another faith by the same Spirit, to another gifts of healing by that one Spirit, to another miraculous powers, to another prophecy, to another distinguishing between spirits, to another speaking in different kinds of tongues, and to still another the interpretation of tongues. All these are the work of one and the same Spirit, and he distributes them to each one, just as he determines. 1 Corinthians 12:7-11

We are supposed to pray to receive these gifts! We can trust God to lead us wisely. We need not lean on our own understanding, but always be aware of God's Word and His goodness, and never do anything that would go against God's Word, such as harming someone else. We are called to love our neighbor as ourselves, including our enemies. We can pray for God to defend us because we are for Him, and of course, He is for us!

What, then, shall we say in response to these things? If God is for us, who can be against us? Romans 8:31

Jesus is the High Priest of the Holy Spirit School of Righteousness, and that's where we want to be. Keep in mind, though, being a disciple of Jesus is a way of life, a life-long process of being refined.

Your ability to humble yourself before God, and go "all in" is the ONLY way this will work. God doesn't want lukewarm disciples. We either learn through lessons, or learn by woe. I prefer to learn by lessons. But even lessons need "field testing" to make sure we really understand the principles, when it comes down to it. Theology is great, but it won't change your life. Christianity is a full-contact sport. You're going to laugh, you are going to cry, and, I promise, you'll spend plenty of time with your face on the ground in prayer.

If you want to experience supernatural miracles and be in the presence of God, you've got to stop flirting with the enemy and be faithful to your God. He deserves it. He's AWESOME. He wants to do amazing things through you and for you, if only you'll turn to Him and stop going your own way. You can't meet Jesus and not be totally transformed by love.

You can't meet Jesus and not be totally transformed by love.

All this "playing church" stuff drives me nuts. I need action, I need intimacy. I'm needy, yes. I want God, and I want Him all the time. It's like I'm in love, and I just can't wait to be with Him. His teachings are invaluable, and life becomes vibrant and new everyday, full of excitement, fulfillment, and love. Of course there are times of pruning, trial, and frustration, but even then, even when the storms make it hard to see where I am going, God is there, leading the way through the muck.

I love to know that I have someone I can totally rely on and trust will always be there. Even the most amazing people will let us down eventually, but God never will. And even if I need

Him in the middle of the night, I can "call" Him; He always answers the phone. He's never too tired, too busy, or annoyed that I call too much. In fact, He is hoping I will call! He's wonderfully compassionate and understanding, but equally terrifying. God's not unlike my husband; he's wonderful and gentle, but I'd never want to mess with him. My husband is tall and strong and commands a certain respect. Not that he demands it or forces it down my throat, but just being in his presence makes a person respect him. That's kind of how it is with God, only a million times more. God is majestic and holy and has armies of angels at His command. He's awesome in so many ways it seems unreal at times because He's just such an incredible God that has so much to offer us, if we would only ask.

I want you to dream with me here for a minute, and dream big, spiritually big. What do you see yourself doing? Close your eyes and think about it. Do you see yourself forgiven, sanctified, glorified, doing something awesome for God? Don't worry if you haven't seen anything yet. Pray for God to open your eyes, and wait for Him to show you. It could take a few hours, days, or even years. If you really want to know, He'll show you. Desperation and thirst are key here. If you really are comfortable in your life, as is, and are not truly ready to make any changes, just put this book back on the shelf. Yoda says, "Do, or do not do. There is no try." There's no in-between. If you are only half doing, or trying, that is not doing.

> *Read the Bible over and over again until you become it, and you'll start to look like Jesus.*

For those of you that are ready to "do," get excited because God is about to do something awesome in your life! Jesus is now your personal High Priest and the Bible is your text book. Read the Bible over and over again until you become it, and you'll start to look like Jesus. Of course there are a ton of lessons you'll want to check out when you are done so be sure to check the Resources section in the back of this book. There are some wonderful free teachings online regarding various spiritual subjects, and I've included notes on some of them so you can check them out.

Try to give yourself a balanced diet of spiritual food, respecting the whole body of Christ in the process, with Jesus, of course, as the head, thinking and directing the way. Put your teaching in His capable hands; He knows you and cares for you. He, alone, knows exactly what you need to become the best you can be. And be patient with yourself; don't beat yourself up about everything, just keep pressing forward, with hope, prayer, and humility.

God's Word is living and active, and it is also timeless. God has the answer to all of our world's problems, if only we would turn to Him instead of psychologists, doctors, teachers, and even politicians. We are a generation of super smart, capable, and gifted people all headed in the wrong direction. Many that "have direction" are going in the wrong direction, working towards fame, fortune, and self-indulgence. They are all working to impress other people instead of aiming to impress God. All these ambitions are powered by the desires of the flesh: the lust of the eyes, the lust of the flesh, and the pride of life. Satan will exploit all these things and try to make you believe that being a Christian is boring and empty and that you'll end up poor and unhappy.

But God's word actually says that God plans to prosper us, to heal every sickness and disease, to bring us into a land flowing with milk and honey. So where is it? That's what spiritual warfare is all about:

That's what spiritual warfare is all about: knocking the lies down as they are shooting at you, and teaching you to grab onto the promises of God and not let go.

knocking the lies down as they are shooting at you, and teaching you to grab onto the promises of God and not let go. First, we need to till some soil, and then we may need to pull a few weeds. Only then can we plant seeds that will grow and mature. And only then will your "fruit" be a benefit to others. I don't want to show you just how to pull weeds. I want to show you how to be free and how to live free, and how to become a real prayer warrior who has an intimate relationship with God, and who knows how to live under the Father's blessings.

I want you to give God one year of your life. Take one year, and make this your number one goal: **To establish and grow a personal relationship with God, making Him #1 in your life.** Just make your #1 goal each day when you get up to be growing closer to God. I personally start and end each day with a devotional like Morning and Evening by Charles Spurgeon, and read the One Year Bible so I can read a little bit each day. Instead of watching TV, I go to YouTube and watch sermons from the teachers I listed in the back of this book.

These tips will help you become an on-fire, Spirit-filled Christian that lives by faith and moves in grace. You will walk in the supernatural and the gifts of the Holy Spirit. You will experience the presence of God and defeat the enemy. You will not be afraid, but rather you will be strong, confident in your relationship with God, and on the narrow path that leads to eternal life. The more you study, pray, fast, and listen to the Holy Spirit, the more authority you will have.

This book can *help* you transform your life, but only if you put your faith in Jesus. I hope that you walk forward with child-like faith, open-minded and ready to receive the word of God for what it actually says, and not what your "experience" (or lack of experience), has already set in your mind. I think what He stands for and what He has planned for you is much more than what you have experienced so far.

There is a lot of literature out there to teach you this or that, but I want to reiterate one thing: this is a written guide, inspired by the Holy Spirit, to guide you in the Ministry of Righteousness. Anything you hear or read, including this book, should be filtered through the Holy Spirit. Ask God if something is true or false and never assume you already know the answer! Good and true things get to go through the filter; bad and false things get rejected and are not allowed to "land".

No spiritual lessons can really be understood the way God intends unless the Holy Spirit is the one explaining it to your heart and spirit. Please don't try to figure some of this stuff out. These are spiritual lessons that need to be discerned through the Spirit.

God's ways are higher than our ways; it's our job to hear Him and obey Him. It's easy once you get the hang of it. Just let go of control; it's totally overrated anyway. And, honestly, you aren't really in control. You are either serving God, or by default, letting yourself be deceived by Satan.

God will do great things with you and expand your influence when you come under His power and desire to be led by His Spirit. His Spirit raised Jesus from the dead; His Spirit parted the Red Sea; His Spirit healed lepers and made the blind see; His Spirit set every captive free from Egypt, and His Spirit wants to live and work through you!

Once you receive power, don't let it go to your head. God doesn't make us healers; He imparts a portion of His Holy Spirit to work through us to heal others. It is always God that performs the miracles; we are, simply, the donkeys carrying the Lord to the people. In God's Kingdom, those that serve will lead. In order to lead God's people, you must learn to follow your Lord Jesus Christ by having intimacy with the Holy Spirit. Getting to know the person of the Holy Spirit is the greatest key to spiritual warfare. The possibilities are literally boundless if you can train yourself to follow Him. All the comfort, guidance, strength, endurance, joy, and spiritual gifts you seek come from Him.

As you begin to really comprehend God's love for you, that love will overflow and you'll start to really love people and see them through God's eyes. You'll have more grace, compassion, patience, and empathy for the world. Naturally, you'll want to help people discover the gift and treasure of having a personal, intimate relationship with their Creator God. As you begin to reach out to people, Christianity will become a lifestyle for you (not just a religion). Praying for people is an honor, but, it is also humbling. Most people are very gracious, but some are very hesitant. Don't ever get tired of doing good; God sees all that you do. We aren't trying to please people; we are acting in love from the thankfulness of what we have received from God.

Whatever you have received from God thus far, there's more. Don't give up, and don't lose hope. I have noticed, with time, miracles become more consistent. I believe this is because our awareness of the Holy Spirit grows, so our faith and confidence grow as well. When you see someone healed from blindness, you are likely to see more people healed because you know for sure that God can *and will* do it! After God healed my spine, I had the opportunity to pray for many people who also received healing in their spine.

When you pray by the leading of the Holy Spirit amazing things will begin to happen. Believe God! All things are possible if you believe! We walk forward with strength, moving from faith to faith, and laughing at what the enemy might try to do to us. We will not be shaken. We are the Bride of Christ; His beloved church. We are clothed with the clean white robes of righteousness, and we walk by faith.

She is clothed with strength and dignity; she can laugh at the days to come. Proverbs 31:25

PRAYERS

You can address your ABBA Father in Heaven in any way that is comfortable for you. I have begun the prayers in various ways to give you examples.

Prayer to Receive Jesus as Your Personal Lord and Savior
Heavenly Father, please forgive me for *all* my sins (take a moment to reflect). I believe that Your Son, Jesus, died for my sins, was buried, and was raised again on the third day. Please come cleanse me from my sins. I give my life to You as a living sacrifice to use as an instrument of righteousness. I turn from my life of sin, and I look to You to lead me. Take the steering wheel of my life and lead me to still waters. Please give me Your Holy Spirit so that I can know you personally. Thank You, Jesus, for taking my place on the cross. Amen!

Prayer for Wisdom and Knowledge
Father God, I ask that you would give me wisdom and knowledge and the spirit of revelation so that I may understand your Word. Thank you, Jesus! Amen.

Prayer for a Discerning Heart and Spiritual Sight
ABBA Father, thank You for Your Son, Jesus, who washed away my sin. Thank you for purifying my spirit and making me a new creation! Please remove this heart of stone, and give me a heart of flesh that hears Your voice. Remove the scales from my eyes so that I may see the beauty and Truth of Your precious Word. Help me to realize the splendor and majesty of who You are. Open my eyes and increase my awareness in knowing when Your angels are working on my behalf. In Jesus Name I pray, Amen.

Prayer for Guidance & Righteousness

Thank You Jesus for making all things new. Thank You for giving me a new spirit. Thank You for forgiving ALL my sins. Thank You, Jesus, for giving me to the power to believe that I am fully forgiven so that I may walk in freedom. Thank You for guiding me with Your Holy Spirit who convicts my heart when I stray from your path. Thank You for giving me the desire to walk in Your ways so that I may have intimacy with You. Remind me daily that I am forgiven, washed, cleansed, sanctified, chosen, set apart, and made holy. Jesus, I give my whole life to You- not just my heart- but all of who I am. Amen!

Prayer to Receive the 7-Fold Spirit of God

Heavenly Father, I praise Your Name and want to glorify You in all that I do. Please give me Your Spirit, and also Wisdom, Understanding, Counsel, Might, Knowledge, and the Fear of the Lord. Father, let me be filled with Your Presence. I dedicate myself to You. Please expand my influence so I can bring glory to Your Kingdom. Teach me Your ways and make me Your bride: perfect, without a spot or wrinkle. Amen!

A shoot will come up from the stump of Jesse; from his roots a Branch will bear fruit. The Spirit of the Lord will rest on him— the Spirit of wisdom and of understanding, the Spirit of counsel and of might, the Spirit of the knowledge and fear of the Lord—and he will delight in the fear of the Lord.
Isaiah 11:1-3

Prayer to Receive the Holy Spirit

Father, thank You for erasing my past. Thank You for making me new. I pray that You would shine light on my whole being. I ask forgiveness for all my sins, and I thank You for the atoning sacrifice of Your Son, Jesus, which cleanses me from all my sin, past, present, and future. I also forgive all others who have sinned against me. I pray for Your mercy, for Your guidance and for Your Holy Spirit. Thank You for giving me Your Holy Spirit. Lead me in Your ways, ABBA, and teach me Your Word. Help me to renew my mind in You, and help me to find time each day so that our relationship can grow. Give me Your understanding and wisdom so that I may know how to apply the teachings to my life, and keep me safe. Thank You for accepting me and loving me, despite my shortcomings and please accept me as a living sacrifice. Mold me into your perfect image. I am Yours, and You are mine. Thank you, Jesus. Amen!

Prayer to Receive Revelation from God

Heavenly Father, thank You for making me Your child! I know I am cleansed and purified thanks to the atoning work of Jesus on the cross. I accept the garments of righteousness, and I want to live for You. I ask You to give me the spirit of wisdom and revelation, so that I may have ears that hear, eyes that see, and a heart that understands. Help me to discern clearly between Your Truth and the lies of the enemy. Use me to bring glory to Your Kingdom and to help others. God thank You for these gifts! Amen.

Prayer to Receive Power and Authority

Heavenly Father, thank You for everything You have given me. I ask now for the power and authority over all demons, and all sickness and disease. I receive this power based on Luke 9 which reads:

When Jesus had called the Twelve together, he gave them power and authority to drive out all demons and to cure diseases, and he sent them out to proclaim the kingdom of God and to heal the sick. Luke 9:1-2

Thank You Jesus that You are my High Priest, and that I am a co-heir with You in the heavenly realm, according to Romans 8:17 which reads:

Now if we are children, then we are heirs—heirs of God and co-heirs with Christ, if indeed we share in his sufferings in order that we may also share in his glory. Romans 8:17

Glory to You, O God! Praise be to You in the highest, forever! Amen!

Prayer for Deliverance

In Jesus's Name, I command the spirit of (blindness, deafness, infirmity, pain, anxiety, depression, death, cancer, etc.; let the Holy Spirit tell you) to leave this body right now! This is a child of God and you have no right to be here! Come out! Jesus, we lift (person's name) up to You. We ask You to heal and restore them. We ask that You would fight spiritually on their behalf. We release Your angels now to help them. We command (parts of the body, such as: head, liver, lungs, spine, foot, etc.) to be healed, in the Name of Jesus! Thank You God! Amen!

Note: After praying for deliverance and/or healing, always check and see how the person feels. You may need to pray once, or it could take a few times depending on the situation.

Prayer for Protection from Witchcraft and Curses

Heavenly Father, In the Name of Jesus, I apply a bloodline of protection around (house, church, school, person, workplace, family, etc.). I lift and remove any curses spoken against them. Please send your angels to protect (house, church, school, person, workplace, family, etc.). Thank You, Jesus, Amen!

Complete Self Deliverance Prayer

I confess Jesus as my Lord and Savior. I believe that You love me, and that You paid the penalty for my sins by dying on the cross, that You, Jesus, were buried and that You were resurrected on the third day. I believe You intercede for me because of my faith in You, and that because I have faith in You, I am saved by grace, and not because I have earned it. I confess faith in being an accepted child of God, and I thank You, Jesus, for Your sacrifice for me. I repent of all my sins (take a moment to reflect on your sins). I forgive ALL who have sinned against me. I forgive (name each person). I renounce all occult activity by myself and/or family members (generational sin). Right now, I lay down pride, bitterness, rebellion, hatred, and all forms of selfishness. Thank You, Jesus, for redeeming me from any curses; I release them now. As a loved child of God, I am now free, and I command all demons to come out now. You no longer have any right to this body, for I am now owned by God. Holy Spirit, I receive You now; come and fill me, equip me, and teach me. Help me to be an instrument of God's love, and conform me into Your perfect image. I welcome Your leadership and I give myself fully to You, Jesus, without reservation. All I have is Yours. Allow me to see, hear, and grow in my personal relationship with You, Jesus. Give me a fire that shines a bright light for You, and help me to keep the fire fed with pure spiritual food. Amen!

Personal/Group
BIBLE STUDY QUESTIONS

Chapter 1: Our Spiritual Foes

1. According the Genesis 1:28, what does God mean by "dominion over the earth"?
2. According to Romans 10:17, how do we get faith?
3. In Matthew 9:35, Jesus goes out to do what two things? How are these two things related?

Chapter 2: Partnering with Heaven

1. According to John 4:28-30, what is the supernatural gift that Jesus used to touch the woman's heart and confirm His authenticity as Messiah?
2. According to Psalm 103:20, what two characteristics are used to describe God's holy angels?
3. In Hebrews 1:14, angels are called "ministering" spirits. What does this mean to you?

Chapter 3: A Defeated Enemy

1. According to John 10:10, what is the devil's plan for you, and what is Jesus's plan for you?
2. According to 1 Kings 3:5-15, why did Solomon ask God for a discerning heart?
3. In James 4:7 what are we told to do before trying to resist the devil or his demons?

Chapter 4: Our Spiritual House

1. According to 1 Corinthians 3:16, where is the Temple of God?
2. After reading this Chapter, is there anything that was brought to your attention?

3. According to Matthew 6:33, what does it mean to "seek first the Kingdom"?

Chapter 5: How to Be Delivered

1. In Matthew 8:16, what happened to the people who came to Jesus? How did He heal them?
2. According to James 4:10, what happens when we humble ourselves to God?
3. According to Mark 16:16, who will be saved?

Chapter 6: Living Victoriously

1. According to Luke 11:24-26, what happens after a person is delivered, if they do not receive the Holy Spirit?
2. According to John 16:33, how do we have peace?
3. According to 1 John 1:5-7, what is the proof that we have fellowship with God?

Chapter 7: Come Under Discipline

1. According to Colossians 3:5-10, what is the reason we should "take off" our old self and "put on" our new self?
2. According to Romans 12:1-2, how can we walk in God's *perfect will*?
3. What are the two things we need to triumph over the enemy according to Revelation 12:11?

Chapter 8: Jesus's Ministry

1. According to Acts 10:38, how was Jesus able to do good and heal people?
2. According to Mark 16:15-18, what signs does Jesus say will accompany those that follow in Him?
3. How does Jesus say that we are going to do "greater things" according to John 14:12?

Chapter 9: His Sheep Know His Voice

1. What promises does Jesus give to His "sheep" according to John 10:7-10?
2. What does 2 Corinthians 10:5 mean by "taking our thoughts captive and making them obedient to Christ"?
3. According to Hebrews 4:16, how can we approach God's throne of grace?

10: Prayer and Powerful Words

1. According to 1 Thessalonians 5:17, how often should we pray?
2. According to 1 Corinthians 12:31, what are we supposed to do regarding spiritual gifts?
3. How do we know what truth to speak over our lives, according to Proverbs 4:20-27?

11: Perfect Faith

1. According to John 16:23-24, what does Jesus tell us the Father will do because of His name?
2. According to James 4:3, what would prevent us from receiving from God?
3. According to Hebrews 12:1-3, how are we encouraged so that we will not become weary?

12: Walking in Authority

1. According to Mark 2:21-22, how do we know that we have authority over demons, sickness, and disease?
2. An angel visits Daniel and says what, according to Daniel 10:18-19?
3. According to Matthew 10:8, what command does Jesus give to His followers?

ADDITIONAL RESOURCES

Still hungry? Check out these ministries on YouTube, or visit their websites for more information and free online teachings. May you seek and find!

William Branham
Todd White
Sid Roth
Derek Prince
Keith Davis
Patricia King
Alan Horvath
Norvel Hayes
Randy Clark
Kathryn Kuhlman
Smith Wigglesworth
Kenneth Hagin

COPYRIGHT INFORMATION

About the Author

Kelly Christina Crumpley lives in Washington State with her husband, David, and has three children. Kelly writes, teaches, speaks, and disciples. Kelly founded Boundless Life Ministries and is working to strengthen the Body of Christ in the areas of the Holy Spirit, Angels, Spiritual Warfare, and Discernment of Spirits. Kelly has had many visions of Jesus, heaven, and has personally experienced the supernatural love and healing touch of God. This is her first book.

A Personal Note to You

I encourage you to hunger and thirst for God. I hope that you'll read this book along with the Bible and apply the teachings of Jesus to your own life. I encourage you to pray for spiritual gifts and the wisdom of God. I pray that you will APPLY the blood covenant of Jesus to your life and walk the way Jesus walked. Renew your mind and be washed clean by God's Living Word. We are called to be a Holy Priesthood. We are not given a spirit of fear, but are called to walk as conquerors in Christ! I know that if God can straighten me out, He can straighten you out too. I know that if I can walk in God's power and authority, you can too. This supernatural life isn't just available to *some* Christians, it is for ALL Christians. Let's change the world together as a united body that seeks intimate fellowship with God, so that we may be a bride without stain or wrinkle. May God's face shine upon you and be gracious to you!

Kelly Crumpley